INSIDE
SCHIZOPHRENIA

INSIDE
SCHIZOPHRENIA

Gwynneth Hemmings

SIDGWICK & JACKSON
LONDON

First published in Great Britain in 1989 by
Sidgwick & Jackson Limited
1 Tavistock Chambers, Bloomsbury Way
London WC1A 2SG

ISBN 0-283-99934-9

Typeset by Hewer Text Composition Services, Edinburgh
Printed by Billings & Son, Worcester

CONTENTS

1

WHAT IS SCHIZOPHRENIA?

My husband's moods were all-important to the rest of the family. I used to watch how the car came into the drive to find out how to deal with him that evening.

If it was driven gently I knew that he would be loving, charming and kind with the children and me. But if the car was reversed sharply up the drive, his face would be red and distraught and he would complain about the children's noise, the mess and the food. He would call me a cow and accuse me of being unfaithful.

Then he would shout, beat up the children if they dropped any food on the floor, lock the eldest one in the broom cupboard, beat me up if I tried to intervene, and punch my stomach and face. . . . After that he would cry, say how sorry he was and ask my forgiveness, then drink himself into a stupor.

My husband gave the impression to the outside world that he was a gentle, loving, hard-working man and that I was a neurotic, crazy woman who lied about what happened in the home. I stayed with him until he lost his temper once too often with my eldest child and tried to strangle him until the boy's face went purple and his eyes bulged out of his head. It took me and both the younger children to get their father off. My husband's eyes were completely enraged, and our voices trying to talk him out of his violence could not penetrate his head.

Seeming normality

That was a courageously written account of the behaviour of an untreated schizophrenic towards his family. The seeming

1

normality displayed by the husband to the outside world is very common in the early stages of the illness.

Swings of mood

The symptoms of schizophrenia come and go, particularly at the start. Thus the wife knew by her husband's driving how he would be that night. If you live with someone whose moods change dramatically you must feel apprehensive at their approach, as this woman was. She might have sweet words or a fight on her hands. She would have to be a saint not to react to her husband's violence, and surely it would become increasingly difficult to react normally when he *was* loving. Could the love be trusted? Or would it give way once again to violence? How long would the period of peace last? How close was the monster lurking behind the kind words?

It was impossible for the wife to know that her husband was developing a severe mental illness, as she had no prior experience of schizophrenia. When her husband eventually attacked one of his workmates he was taken to hospital and injected with anti-schizophrenic drugs, after which his mental condition greatly improved. But by then his wife had divorced him.

An inherited disease

Schizophrenia is an inherited disease (see Chapter 3) that can, and often does, wreck the life of the patient and destroy his or her family. Once it was called madness, a robust term that everyone understood. But in the 1880s a German psychiatrist, Dr Emil Kraepelin, started calling it dementia praecox, meaning 'madness of the young'. This term was not, however, to last for long, for just before the First World War Dr Eugen Bleuler, a Swiss psychiatrist, renamed it with the current term, schizophrenia, which means 'split mind'. Emotions appear to override the intellect preventing it from functioning normally.

Different effects on men and women

The disease occurs in about 1 per cent of the population worldwide, although there are geographical variations where the incidence is higher or lower. Men and women appear to be affected in equal numbers, although men seem to suffer an earlier onset and a more severe form of the disease. Onset is usually at adolescence or early adulthood (hence 'madness of the young'). It is thought that certain female hormones – oestrogens – may protect younger women against the more severe aspects of the disease. When production of these hormones diminishes at the time of the menopause, however, women's symptoms may increase.

Personality change

At present, schizophrenia means many things to many people. To the patient and his family it is often hell on earth. It is so frightening and so overwhelming because it affects the brain chemistry and thus – often insidiously – it alters the behaviour, thoughts and emotions of the person developing the disease. He is no longer the person he was, which is a terrible shock to everyone concerned. Thus a kind, loving husband and father can turn into the brutal, violent person described at the beginning of this chapter.

The three major symptoms

Schizophrenia has many symptoms at its various stages, but what are known as the three major first-rank symptoms are delusions, hallucinations and thought disorder. Varying expressions of these and other symptoms can be seen in the case histories in this chapter.

Superhuman strength

Robert Burton, author of *The Anatomy of Melancholy*, wrote this interesting account of the condition in the 1660s:

> Madness is therefore defined to be a vehement dotage, or raving without a fever far more violent than melancholy [depression], full of anger and clamour, horrible looks, actions, gestures troubling the patients with far greater vehemency both of

3

body and mind without all fear and sorrow, with such impetuous force and boldness that sometimes three or four men cannot hold them, blood incensed and brains inflamed.

In both Burton's account and that of the wife which opened this chapter, the person affected is described as phenomenally strong. This is a well-known fact, for which science has as yet discovered no reason.

Lack of remorse

It is also widely accepted that such people rarely show remorse ('without all fear and sorrow', as Burton calls it). In the wife's account the husband was still sufficiently in contact with reality to ask her forgiveness after he had got over a violent attack. But very often, as the disease develops, such a sense of conscience is not shown. The press frequently contains reports of prisoners in the dock who are said by the judge to show no remorse for their violent actions: these individuals are often unrecognized cases of schizophrenia. Peter Sutcliffe, the Yorkshire Ripper, felt fully justified in killing prostitutes because God had told him to do so. He showed no remorse and said he was acting in response to his 'voices'. Sutcliffe was not an inherently evil man, as the press and jury thought, but a severely ill schizophrenic suffering from auditory hallucinations (see p. 7) on which he acted.

The poet Robert Browning understood madness very well. In 'Porphyria's Lover', Porphyria is murdered by her lover whilst she still worships him:

> That moment she was mine, mine, fair
> Perfectly pure and good. I found
> A thing to do, and all her hair
> In one long yellow string I wound
> Three times her little throat around
> And strangled her. No pain felt she
> I am quite sure she felt no pain.
> And all night long we have not stirred
> And yet God has not said a word!

Again there is no remorse and no realization of the enormity of the crime. Porphyria's lover is depicted as being in a gentle and happy mood, thinking he has preserved, through death, someone who greatly loves him. Today we learn through the media of mothers who have killed their children (and sometimes themselves) to protect them in similar fashion from the unknowable future, full of imagined terrors thought up by their deluded minds.

Suicides

Porphyria's lover is perhaps not too dissimilar to Ophelia in *Hamlet*. He in his madness makes his violence seem quite normal. Ophelia's violence is to herself – one of the major tragedies of schizophrenia is the great number of suicides and attempted suicides which occur as a result of disturbed brain chemistry.

Thought disorder

Laertes, Ophelia's brother, says she 'speaks things in doubt that carry but half sense . . . which as her winks and nods and gestures yield, then indeed would make one think there would be thought'. Ophelia was suffering from thought disorder. She only makes 'half sense' and sometimes utters – in a very matter-of-fact way – nonsensical statements like: 'They say the owl was a baker's daughter.'

Thought disorder may take various forms, ranging from what is known as word salad (a complete and pretty meaningless collection of spoken words) to a blank mind. One woman told me how awful it was when she had no thoughts in her head. It frightened her greatly, and when a single thought came to her it was a considerable relief. How often this occurs I do not know, but some schizophrenics sit for long periods doing and saying nothing. Whether they are listening to their 'voices' (see p. 7) or whether their minds are blank it is impossible to know. At times some patients believe that thoughts are being withdrawn from their brains by an external agency.

Shakespeare's Ophelia also speaks in verse, which is a common

symptom. A more modern 'schizophrenic poet' of my acquaintance spoke with sweet smiles and gestures, just like Ophelia,
as he walked hand in hand with his children in the sunshine
– saying everything in rhyme. The gentleness eventually gave
way to violence, and he shouted at the daily cleaner: 'How dare
you have a yellow bucket, woman!' He hurled her bucket away
and started to strut about with accentuated prancing movements,
eyes closed, face fierce and hands together in prayer. Eventually
his shouting and praying turned to groans; he closed the shutters
against the sun and lay down in the dark.

Delusions of persecution (paranoia)

Patients suffering from delusions are not susceptible to rational
argument. A man once came to consult me totally convinced
that his workmates were out to do him down. His brother,
who accompanied him, assured me that this was completely
untrue. For hours my husband and I talked with the deluded
man to try to persuade him that his beliefs were false, but to
no avail.

Another patient wrote to me about her delusions of persecution: 'For some years I refused to leave the house unless I was
armed with several knives, and this led to me feeling tormented
by the thought that I might actually wound and kill someone.'
How she must have suffered doubly, from fear of what others
might do to her and she to them.

Obsessive suspicion of others – paranoia – which so often results
in violence as a defence mechanism, must surely be the symptom
of schizophrenia people most fear. This description of her son
was sent to me by a member of The Schizophrenia Association
of Great Britain. It is quite typical of the behaviour of a severe
paranoid schizophrenic (see p. 10) who is untreated.

I think one of the most overwhelming emotions he feels is fear
– fear of all manner of things. For example, he is obsessed with
security and locks. This flat is like Fort Knox. There are locks
and bolts on all the windows.

He had a nasty habit of coming up to within two or three

inches of me, then forcing me to walk backwards around the flat until we reached the top of our steep flight of stairs. Then he'd laugh a nasty laugh and say 'Why don't you throw yourself down there?' It happened often. Later I'd find myself pinned in a corner with both his fists quivering in my face. 'I'll beat you to a pulp,' he'd say. 'I'll break your bones. You know I could do it, too, don't you?'

I can't stand threats now, or bullying, or fists flashing past my face, or his grabbing my arm or ankle and threatening to break it.

He has an enormous appetite, and when he's hungry he's very aggressive. Quote: 'I'm hungry. I'm almost homicidal.' After he's had a meal he calms down.

Delusions of grandeur

If delusions of persecution seem tragic, then delusions of grandeur can sometimes appear comic – though they are no less distressing in their way. One man, believing himself to be King of Wales, brought his regalia to court when up on a minor charge.

Hallucinations

Caused by abnormal perceptions, hallucinations may take many forms and are the cause of much anguish. They are apparently less common amongst paranoid schizophrenics than amongst non-paranoid ones (see p. 10).

Auditory hallucinations

These are probably the most frightening type of hallucination, for real voices seem to speak out loud inside the patient's head. They may order him to do things, or comment on him unpleasantly and endlessly. Sometimes patients may answer their voices back or giggle at what they say. Recently I heard of a schoolteacher who bravely goes on teaching despite the voices in his head. How many people suffer these voices unknown to anyone else? How many, like Joan of Arc or Peter Sutcliffe, act on the commands of their voices?

Apart from voices in the head, the perception of external sound is altered for these patients. For example, someone may be speaking several rooms away and yet the patient can hear his words; and if the radio is on at ordinary volume, it may seem excessively loud. On the other hand, patients often play very loud music in order to drown their voices. Sometimes patients think that people on the television are speaking specially to them. It can be difficult for someone with schizophrenia to speak with a group of people or in a crowd; the patient is unable to concentrate, and all sorts of other sounds distract him, particularly since they may seem very loud.

Visual hallucinations

The hallucinations may be visual, in which case the patient sees people and scenes which are not there. At other times there are more concrete altered perceptions. One young woman wrote: 'Objects appeared to move and I often felt that the floors and walls were breathing, which I could actually see and hear.' Occasionally patients cannot stand daylight, especially if it is bright (like the man in the 'yellow bucket' story) – it appears to cause actual physical pain.

Hallucinations of smell and taste

One woman patient came into our house and said she could smell toast burning. Yet no toast or any other food was being cooked at the time.

A number of patients think their food is being poisoned because it tastes different. One patient, believing something had been put in his tea, decided to have his revenge in like manner. He picked some poisonous yew twigs and made a brew of them with water, ready to give to the suspected poisoner. Luckily he was taken to hospital before any harm was done.

Acknowledging violence as a symptom

Violence may seem to have loomed large in my description of schizophrenia. In many books this symptom is played down, but in reality it is the most frightening aspect of the disease. Many doctors seem not to want to know, or may perhaps deliberately conceal violence, thinking that by so doing the stigma attached to schizophrenia may be reduced. But to hide a serious symptom like violence is to run away from reality, and is likely only to increase the stigma – in a furtive way. Truth is the only way to progress, and if the symptoms are awful they must be admitted to be so.

Most frequently, as with the wife whose story opened this chapter, it is those nearest and dearest to the patient who receive the brunt of the assaults. I remember vividly a man who rushed into our house one evening, having travelled all day to get there. He was terrified that he would harm one of his children. By about midnight I was able to get the police and an ambulance to take him to the nearest psychiatric hospital – from which, to my amazement, he was allowed home two days later. Not long afterwards he did attempt to drown one of his children; as a result he spent the rest of his life either in prison or in hospital, where he eventually killed himself.

His wife was broken-hearted. She wrote again and again to tell me what a wonderful husband and father he had been and how great his love was for them all. It is a major tragedy when a man like that tries to get help, but finds it is in vain.

One young mother read of another woman killing her children and thought to herself, in terrible anguish, 'How am *I* different?' The fear gripped her all day long but disappeared if she woke during the night. The next day, however, the thoughts would return with all their fearfulness. Had she been given appropriate medication these thoughts would rapidly have been replaced by normal ones.

Stereotyped behaviour

Another typical symptom is stereotyped behaviour. A patient may play the same tune on the piano over and over again, or listen to the same tape, or read the same book. One patient often played very loudly, in the middle of the night, a record of Kathleen Ferrier singing Brahms's *Alto Rhapsody*. It may have been a source of comfort to a very ill, isolated man, but to his wife it brought tremendous fear. Even now, when her husband is well again, a few bars of the *Alto Rhapsody* give her a panicky feeling.

Inappropriate emotions

In his autobiography, *Memoirs of a Thinking Radish*, the scientist Sir Peter Medawar described his brother's manic laughter, which embarrassed him greatly when he was dining with him in his London club. Many schizophrenics display inappropriate emotions, but in different ways. They may be sad and weep profusely for no apparent reason, or they may become angry and quarrel without cause. Very often the mood accompanying paranoia may be acute anxiety or depression, and patients lose their natural warmth and spontaneity. They may laugh unnaturally at sad events, and look poker-faced and glum at an entertainment where everyone else is laughing. One schizophrenic husband said to his wife: 'The only emotion I can make you feel is fear.' It was perhaps his own chief emotion, which he was projecting on to his wife.

Our emotions are influenced by hormones, and in schizophrenia it is likely that the hormonal systems are upset. Untreated schizophrenics rarely look or feel happy, unless they are in a manic mood – and then it is not real happiness. This is one of the saddest aspects of the disease: it is tragic when a patient is unable to feel pleasure – a condition known as anhedonia.

Paranoid and non-paranoid schizophrenia

There are moves within psychiatry to make a clear distinction between paranoid and non-paranoid schizophrenia, for the problems of each type seem to be of a very different nature. The more extreme of the symptoms described above belong to paranoid schizophrenia. Without the elements of paranoia and hostility, schizophrenia becomes an altogether milder and less ominous problem – the other symptoms, such as reclusiveness, lack of communication, depression and thought disorder, are not in themselves to be feared. Non-paranoid schizophrenia is subdivided into simple, *hebephrenic* (*hebe* – blunt; *phrenic* – mind; therefore blunt mind) and *catatonic* (*cata* – ceasing; *tonic* – muscle tone; therefore lack of muscle tone) forms.

Simple non-paranoid schizophrenia

This form has a gradual onset and starts in the young. Previously the patient may have been intelligent and stable, but now he becomes increasingly ineffective, solitary or apathetic, and perhaps depressed. There are apparently no delusions or hallucinations, and therefore there is no break with reality. Simple schizophrenia has been described as a 'state of apathy and contentment where the patient has no ambition or any great capacity for enjoying himself, nor any appreciation that he is ill'. Such patients do not fulfil their early promise, but their memory remains good. They can seem a bit simple and smile foolishly, and there may be evidence of self-neglect.

Simple schizophrenia may well be related to paranoid schizophrenia, as the two seem to occur in different members of the same family. Their problems are in no way the same, but their medical solutions may be the same or similar.

Hebephrenic non-paranoid schizophrenia

Here the onset is quite sudden, which distinguishes it from the paranoid and simple non-paranoid forms. The hebephrenic form is characterized by thought disorder and inappropriate emotions – incoherent talk, laughter and giggling for no apparent cause, and wild excitement. Occasional sudden outbursts of violent anger are not usually long-lasting. Sometimes vivid visual and auditory hallucinations are present. There are delusions but, unlike those of paranoid schizophrenia, they are not fixed and may be of a fantastic rather than a persecutory nature.

I have seldom come across a case of hebephrenic schizophrenia, which is quite rare. So this example of the way a typical hebephrenic patient talks comes from D. F. Henderson and R. D. Gillespie's *Textbook of Psychiatry* (1937):

I don't like acting the goat at all. A cream sponge sandwich. My memory is so slow, that's all, I'm sure. It was caramels and fruit cakes. Well, well, I said, I can't help it – I don't want to help it and, well, I don't care. Contrary Mary again and says – Nurse Grant – dogs barking. What's the matter with me, that's all. Sago pudding. She looks pale and tired often, but no – I know that. Dear God. I am so silly. It's killing, isn't it? Cream cakes, French cakes and meringues. Flies, fleas, butterflies.

Catatonic non-paranoid schizophrenia

Mysteriously, this sub-group appears to have almost disappeared from the West, although it is still common in North Africa and other areas of the Third World. It was, however, common in the United Kingdom when Henderson and Gillespie's book was written, and here is their description:

A general falling off of interest, apathy; a lack of concentration, a dreaminess and often episodes of an odd nature. Then a state of dull stupor develops, with mutism, refusal of food, and with such a diminution of all activities that the patient may sit idly in one position, with the hands stretched out on his knees, and the head bowed between the shoulders, the whole aspect being that of a mummy. The facial expression is vacant and no apparent interest is taken in the environment or the people around. The muscles of the mouth become pursed up. Patients in this condition have to be dressed and undressed and have to be moved in bed. For months on end they have to be tube-fed. Urine and faeces are often retained or there is incontinence. They do however understand perfectly clearly everything that is going on around them.

The problems of wrong diagnosis

The presence of thought disorder, hallucinations and delusions (the three major first-rank symptoms) are thought by most psychatrists to be essential before a diagnosis of schizophrenia can be made. Chapter 2, however, will explain that they are by no means the only important symptoms of the disease – neither are they exclusive to it. A patient suffering from tertiary syphilis in the old days might have been indistinguishable from one suffering from schizophrenia; so too, nowadays, may someone with a *toxic psychosis*. A toxic psychosis is a psychosis caused by toxins (poisons) produced for example by a focus of infection – as in say appendicitis. Such toxins can produce mental symptoms. Likewise people can hallucinate if they drink too much alcohol or take certain street drugs such as LSD or amphetamines.

In addition, the symptoms by which schizophrenia is usually diagnosed may be the last ones to appear in a disease which has been developing for many years. Bleuler, the coiner of the term 'schizophrenia', certainly believed so: 'The disease itself, even when far advanced,' he wrote, 'need not produce any of the symptoms commonly considered as typical.'

Outcome

There is often discussion about outcome of the disease and figures are given for how many patients recover; how many stay half-well and half-ill and how many become very deteriorated. Largely I think the outcome is dependent on the skill of the psychiatrist in treating the patient and in his belief that he can get rid of the psychosis. No psychiatrist should give up with any case of schizophrenia however refractory to treatment it appears to be. It is no good for psychiatrists to turn to the parents of a patient, as they do, and say: 'You may as well forget him. He'll never get any better.' Or: 'The outlook is hopeless.' These are indeed counsels of despair and should never be considered. Psychiatrists who believe in a wholly medical model for schizophrenia are likely to be those who succeed in getting their patients well. If the disease is adequately and skilfully treated the patient has every chance, even in our present limited state of knowledge, of living a satisfactory and happy life. A consideration of outcome is pessimistic. I know of at least two cases of severely ill schizophrenics who moved to another area, thus coming under the care of another psychiatrist. They became wonderfully better to the joy of their relatives.

Dr Ming T. Tsuang (1982), a psychiatrist, has recently said that *what schizophrenia is* 'depends upon the definition of characteristic features of schizophrenia' and that 'seventy years after Bleuler first used the word, there is still no unanimously accepted definition of schizophrenia.' For researchers into the biochemistry of the disease this is a very uneasy conclusion.

Hope for the future

More positively, these brain symptoms may prove to be the most fleeting once we know better how to control the disease. I am encouraged to think in this way by the occasional report from the psychiatric profession that suddenly, with an unusual (and perhaps potentially harmful) treatment, like the drug sodium amytal, the real personality of a patient has briefly returned. Even that fleeting glimpse – for perhaps only half a day – is, however, enough to give us reason to hope that the brain is not damaged in schizophrenia, but that toxins merely envelop it and disturb its delicate biochemistry.

References

HENDERSON, D. K. & GILLESPIE, R. D. (1937): *A Textbook of Psychiatry*. Oxford Medical Publications.
TSUANG, MING T. (1982): *Schizophrenia, The Facts*. Oxford University Press.

2

THE EARLY SYMPTOMS

What alarm and distress could be saved if the violence of temper of commencing brain disease were regarded with physiological clarity and properly treated. How much mental illness could be avoided if its causes were understood and its preliminary symptoms properly treated. The beginnings of evil are always the most difficult to detect. Advanced evils are easy enough to diagnose.

Those were the words of T. E. Clouston, an eminent psychiatrist working at the beginning of the twentieth century in the Royal Edinburgh Hospital for the Insane.

Early diagnosis

With schizophrenia, as with cancer, early diagnosis is of paramount importance if the condition is to be held in check. In families with a history of mental illness doctors should be looking for the early signs of schizophrenia, and not waiting for the last symptoms to arrive – yet despite Dr Clouston's words, written nearly a century ago, few of them seem to do so. We asked members of the Schizophrenia Association of Great Britain how much time had elapsed between their realization that something was wrong with a member of their family and the time when schizophrenia was diagnosed. The average was about three years.

In the interim, while the disease was developing insidiously, attempts were being made by doctors to give some sort of diagnosis. Over a quarter of the patients were told they had a personality disorder; just under 4 per cent were given a diagnosis of psychopathic disorder.

Summary of wrong diagnoses

Other diagnoses mentioned were:

- Depression
- Temporal lobe (of the brain) epilepsy
- Nervous debility
- Schizoid personality
- Identity crisis
- Psychosomatic disorder
- Paraphrenic illness
- Adolescent turmoil
- Thought disorder
- Neurosis
- Stress reaction
- Lack of social life
- 'My brain was ill'
- Too high a dose of steroids
- Delusional psychosis
- Schizo-affective disorder
- Behavioural problems
- Progressive nervous disease
- Low blood sugar
- Anxiety
- Manic depression
- Post-natal depression

Anxiety and depression are often found accompanying schizo-phrenia, and they will respond to treatment with neuroleptic (anti-schizophrenic) medication if they are present before more florid symptoms. But most doctors seem to regard them as diagnoses in themselves, rather than as symptoms of another disease.

Some of these alternative diagnoses may even have been given *after* an initial diagnosis of schizophrenia, as in a case I heard of recently. Four years after schizophrenia had been diagnosed by two psychiatrists, a woman patient was told by a third psychiatrist that she was suffering from personality disorder.

Doctors are extremely unwilling to make an overt diagnosis of schizophrenia, particularly at an early stage in its course. Yet specialists in other fields are very eager to diagnose early, so that treatment can start. They do not wait for a tumour to grow large before they operate, and they aim to identify early malignancies of the cervix by screening women regularly. Why, then, do they not adopt the same approach to schizophrenia? Why do they wait for years before initiating treatment, while the family may be suffering intensely?

To be fair, the situation is perhaps not as easy for psychiatrists as for GPs. They did not know the patient when he was well, and so they cannot appreciate the slow but tremendous changes in personality which have taken place while the disease has been developing. As one psychiatrist said: 'Intelligent schizophrenics are very good at hiding their symptoms.'

Bodily degeneration

Morel, a French psychiatrist working in the middle of the last century, stressed that bodily degeneration was the basis of hereditary mental disease. But most psychiatrists today believe that schizophrenia is confined to the brain, and that the brain symptoms are the only ones that count. Unlike the old doctors, they do not look for earlier physical signs which might be the precursors of the brain symptoms.

Loss of weight

Clouston described a twenty-three-year-old male patient's illness and his treatment of it (no neuroleptic drugs were available to him in those days):

In 1898 a young man had been working extra hard to pass an examination. He lost his power to sleep, got restless, talkative, violent and unmanageable at home. His temperature was 100.1;

17

his pulse 84 and weak; his weight 11st 12lb. He was kept outside [in the asylum] in [the] charge of two good attendants, though most violent.

He was compelled to take four custards a day, each containing four eggs and a pint and a half of milk, in addition to any ordinary food he could be got to take. He was treated with warm baths at night; with cold to his head and large doses of bromide and iodide of potassium combined while the temperature was high. He slept little and in spite of enormous quantities of nourishment taken he fell off in flesh and strength. In the first six weeks of his stay in the asylum he lost 28lb in weight. . . . The nourishment was made a little more stimulating by strong soups. He got fresh vegetables, cod-liver oil with the hypophosphates and strychnine and iron.

He was narrowly watched and well nursed. . . . He slowly picked up flesh and his beard and whiskers began to sprout. I have much faith in adolescent recoveries when the beard grows coincidentally with recovery – and his weight increased fast and steadily until six months from the commencement of his illness he was quite well in mind. Unfortunately he relapsed after a while.

Another patient was a brilliant student. 'His heredity,' said Clouston, was

very neurotic, mother being very nervous, aunt insane and father drunken. Without any proximate cause he became much exalted in mind and much excited, sleepless and fell off his food . . . when he came to the asylum he was quite incoherent, raving about religion and women. His tongue and lips were dry; his temperature 99 degrees, pulse 144 small and thready, and his general strength small, though his maniacal muscular energy was great.

I could get him to take no food, so at once fed him with the stomach pump. He had to be put in the padded room at night on account of his delirious violence, but was taken out each day into the fresh air by three good attendants. . . . His bodily health and strength gradually improved; his beard and whiskers sprouted in great luxuriance but his mental powers did not return. He continued to write poetry but it got more and more incoherent.

The process of fattening such a patient and the conditions under which it takes place are antagonistic to the disease and its results. It is common to gain a stone a month. I believe that by a proper diet and regimen along with other means, we can fight against and counteract inherited neurotic tendencies in children and tide them over the periods of puberty and adolescence.

Obviously Clouston understood the physical nature of the disease and the fact that the special nourishment given to the patient improved both his body and his brain. Loss of weight is a common early sign of severe schizophrenia.

Clouston's descriptions can be compared with this present-day account by Ami S. Brodoff of her schizophrenic brother, published in the *Schizophrenia Bulletin* series of first-person accounts in 1988. Her brother became

More troubled and dishevelled than usual. He was still handsome but too thin now, unkempt. He had trouble engaging in any sustained conversation and frequently needed to withdraw. . . . I found him wearing a pair of gloves, frantically brushing at his clothes as though trying to rid himself of a swarm of clinging insects. The sight of a spider had convinced him that a vast colony of insects was quietly weaving *his* web. Black ants, beetles, gnats and fluttering moths had teemed on, he believed, fastening themselves to the web – a cage that threatened to imprison him.

The writer was astounded to look back at photographs of him when he was young and apparently healthy, to discover that he had exhibited physical symptoms even then. She described him in these words:

He holds his body in an odd concave position, sucking in the centre of his body with his head pitched awkwardly forward. Thin arms bent at the elbow, hanging lank behind his torso as if he holds on to a set of invisible supporting bars. Occasionally he smiles but these pictures are the most disturbing of all. My brother's taut, clenched smile, baring most of his upper and lower front teeth, conveys only great tension and pain.

The problems of untrained carers

One important point to emerge from Clouston's accounts is that either two or three attendants looked after a single patient. Nowadays, if similar severely ill patients refuse to accept treatment in an institution because they do not believe they are ill, they are cared for at home – usually by non-professionals. Not only are their families not trained to look after the mentally sick, but they are frequently not physically strong enough for the task. The more ill a schizophrenic is, the less likely he is to appreciate that he is ill at all. As the patient is often extremely paranoid towards his closest relatives, this makes it very much harder for them to help as they would want to. It can also put them at risk.

Poor posture

The young man whose symptoms are next described tragically committed suicide. He was diagnosed as manic depressive, but since a number of patients who are SAGB members are given both diagnoses at different stages in their disease, by different psychiatrists, and as there is a growing acceptance that manic depression may be a different phase of schizophrenia, I include his story here.

Pure white hair at birth and *very* exceptionally fair until eight or ten, thereafter remaining blond. Could this be zinc deficiency?

Occasional fits of uncontrollable temper, at the same time showing abnormal strength.

Most important, strange position of neck in photograph taken a year before illness was recognized and in a subsequent one during illness. The head was pushed backwards and tilted upwards, maybe to relieve pressure. (Sheep have been observed to do this while suffering from hypoglycaemia [low blood sugar]). We sought medical advice for this condition. Acute diarrhoea in infancy (four to five months); impetigo aged about ten; terrible boil-like spots on back ('Just part of the problems of adolescence,' I was told); anxiety over difficulties in expressing himself fluently in speech.

Again, this was a very interesting account by an observant and knowledgeable mother. The pure white hair could have been a melanin (pigmentation) deficiency. The posture of schizophrenics is often exceptionally poor, leading to poor lung functioning, and in this respect the description is similar to the previous one.

Other common early symptoms

The concentration of younger schizophrenics often falls off and they are consequently unable to study, whether at school or college. Their handwriting frequently deteriorates dramatically and may be very tiny, or scrawly and barely legible – it is often possible to make an accurate guess at the state of a patient's health from his handwriting alone. Students who become ill may be criticized for allowing their standards to fall. They may feel extremely tired during the day and become over-active at night. They may exhibit increased irritability, aggression, bad temper, hostility and violence without cause.

A number of the symptoms described in Chapter 1 can appear at this time. Very often the patient projects his own feelings on to those closest to him, and alienates himself from them. Eventually he will become isolated and very lonely. He will be uncommunicative and reply in monosyllables, or rage and storm. He may eat alone, fearing his food is poisoned. The patient may feel physically hurt by bright light. Ordinary sounds may appear deafeningly loud, and hurt the patient's ears.

Unfortunately all these symptoms, both behavioural and physical, may be ignored if the patient goes to the doctor. All too often they will be attributed to growing pains or the problems of adolescence.

Body temperature and skin

Schizophrenics may have increased skin coloration and look suntanned in the middle of winter; alternatively their skin can look translucent or ashen. They may sweat profusely – with

a characteristic and unusual aromatic smell – and have poor cir-
culation, which will result in cold hands and feet. One patient said
his bones felt so cold he thought he would never get warm again,
and an SAGB member wrote to me about his severe coldness in
the early hours of the morning, calling it 'the dawn peak'. Thirty
per cent of a sample of forty-four Schizophrenia Association of
Great Britain members were found to suffer from hypothermia.

Digestive problems

Modern psychiatrists do not ask their patients if they have digestive problems (see Chapter 7), even though historically their presence was well known. Sickness, diarrhoea, colic and constipation
are all common. Aches and pains may rack the body of the patient,
and yet are often ignored by the doctor and dismissed as being 'all
in the mind'.

Some while ago SAGB members were asked if the schizophrenic
patient in the family had any digestive problems. Out of 253
returned questionnaires, 108 mentioned problems of this kind.
Many had started when the patient was a baby, and the replies
included:

● Severe stomach pains as a young child and diarrhoea frequently
in the mornings
● Mother had trouble finding the right food to suit me when I
was a baby
● As a child suffered from acidosis, as did sister, mother and
mother's sister
● Acidosis as a young baby and young child
● Allergic to milk as a baby – acidosis as a child, and occasionally
still
● As a baby, very difficult to feed after weaning
● From babyhood until present, allergic to milk
● Gastroenteritis on and off since a baby – epidemic in the hospital
when born
● Immediately after birth, vomited violently after breast-feeding
● Renal colic and acidosis as a baby. Later, pain like gall-bladder
trouble

● As a baby, brought back food to an alarming degree

These first symptoms may hold vital clues to the development of the illness. A very high rate of feeding difficulties became evident, and milk is certainly a suspect food.

Looking backward in the history of schizophrenic illnesses

The distinction has to be made between schizophrenia which starts in childhood and that which starts in adolescence or later and which may have had childhood symptoms which only assume significance in retrospect. I will describe the latter first.

The following case histories describe the actual early behaviour of those who later became schizophrenic. They are remembered by parents, mostly mothers, who may also have had children who did not develop schizophrenia, and with whom they could compare the child who became ill. Such behaviour, whilst perhaps not unusual in isolation, could become so when looked at as a group of behaviours which became significant in retrospect. These children described *did* become schizophrenic as adults and we are looking now for patterns of behaviour which might in some cases be significant. They might become useful pointers to those who seek to prevent the development of a schizophrenic illness early in its course. Unless we know these early behaviours we will not recognize them as perhaps symptomatic in some instances.

We asked SAGB members to tell us what early isolated and sporadic symptoms they had noticed in the schizophrenic person in their family before the onset of the full-blown illness. Our aims were the same as those of D. K. Henderson and R. D. Gillespie in the 1930s, whose *Textbook of Psychiatry* we quoted:

We believe therefore that closer attention should be paid to obtaining very complete records of the development of the patient and that the idiosyncrasies and perversities of childhood be scanned with more seriousness, because by doing so we may be able to determine traits which are likely to be followed by more serious symptoms that only become significant in

23

retrospect, perhaps an abnormal behaviour or a reversal of previously held beliefs or physical symptoms.

One mother wrote to me about her daughter, whose behaviour was severely disturbed. She had been seeing a therapist – probably a psychologist – for some while. I suggested she should ask for her daughter to be given a neuroleptic drug. In a subsequent letter the mother said that a neuroleptic had indeed been prescribed after she had shown my letter to the therapist and consultant. She told me that it was 'making so much difference to the family – less anger and more mixing'. Whereas previously the daughter had smashed china whenever a visitor came, now she would sit and chat to them. 'Isn't it a pity,' wrote the mother, 'that four years of her life have gone by when so much suffering for us all could have been relieved? Many times I've phoned the hospital in utter despair, and all I got told was "Go out for a walk and calm down."' There must be countless patients who could easily be helped, as this girl was, by a small dosage of medication and an overt diagnosis of schizophrenia when their behaviour has altered markedly for no apparent reason.

Another mother wrote:

She had always been very independent, even as a little girl. We were somewhat amused, and felt that it was good as she would evidently be able to stand on her own feet. However, this turned into signs of withdrawal from the family as she entered her teens and she began to get very wilful. It was viewed by doctors as adolescence or artistic temperament, even though it was a complete change from her basic character, which was loving, caring and family-centred.

She attended lessons in natural movement and ballet from the age of about eight to fourteen, and she much enjoyed them. Her teachers often remarked to me that she was most helpful with the little ones. At this time she had a full and happy life and school was no problem. She won a scholarship at eleven. At thirteen, not long after puberty, her form-mistress told us she was disappointed at her change of companions in class – she was getting friendly with the time-wasters and rebels instead of the industrious girls with whom she had previously associated.

24

But she continued to do well at her school work. She was also good at sport and swam for the school, so it was felt she was very well balanced.

Although she was sometimes difficult and secretive it was only intermittent until she went to college, when she became more of a stranger. But this we accepted, with regret, as 'growing up' – and the sixties was, after all, a very permissive time! On one of her visits home she wept a lot and was in a state of depression. . . . Apparently she had become pregnant, and termination had been arranged. She carried this 'guilt' with her for years and had her beautiful hair cut off as a 'penance'. But it was a long time before she told us about it.

After her graduation she was offered a teaching post for one year and happily accepted it, but schizophrenia was already on her and, although her teaching was good, she was utterly unreliable. Since her behaviour was getting worse the contract was not renewed. I visited her several times while she was teaching. She was always wanting money, and I remember how shaky her hands were and how unnaturally bright her eyes. This was later assumed to be drugs, but no doubt it was schizophrenia. Also, she could never keep an appointment. Several times I arranged to meet her and she didn't turn up. Usually she had quite forgotten and was still in bed.

She had two further pregnancies and terminations, one after she had absconded from a psychiatric hospital and gone missing in London for ten days. After eight months at that hospital she was far worse than she had ever been. Years later I found that the treatment had been psychoanalytic – it nearly destroyed both her and us. After absconding from the hospital she arrived at our home pregnant, gaunt and filthy, like someone out of Belsen.

The mother added a final comment to her account: 'The main points I wanted to make were the emotional instability, the trembling and shaky hands, the big mood swing from being loving to being hard and intolerant, tearful, forgetful and utterly improvident, i.e. buying expensive new shoes when there was nothing to eat.'

This story, written by a very brave mother, graphically describes her daughter's early history, which is fairly typical of one sort of schizophrenia in women. The secrecy, promiscuity and improvidence may not be considered symptoms at all, yet they do contribute to the picture of the illness; promiscuity may be a common feature of the female schizophrenic.

In the next case history a mother describes her son, whose father went into hospital with schizophrenia when the boy was seven.

> I feared for my son, though he did not give any cause for alarm until he was nineteen. Until then he had been what you might call a model son, good-natured, affectionate, a good mixer with others, very considerate and very studious (he had a very high IQ), and he did not exhibit anything abnormal. But at nineteen he developed a bad temper and became destructive. I noticed a slowing down of activity, physical and mental. He took a teaching post. On holiday with me he confided that he had hallucinations and some obsessive habits. He gave up teaching and shut himself away in a cottage he had bought. Here he tried to live on very little money and became like something out of Belsen. Nothing I could do or say would alter his attitude. When we managed to get him into hospital schizophrenia was diagnosed.

Thin and poorly muscled bodies

In both these case histories the mother spoke of the schizophrenic son or daughter as looking emaciated, like an inmate of the Belsen concentration camp. This is highly significant in the light of Clouston's descriptions of weight loss in patients. In her book *The Schizophrenic Child* (1982) Dr Sheila Cantor has described muscle loss in such children. This is perhaps the most consistent feature of many early schizophrenic adults, particularly the paranoid ones, who have what is called an asthenic build – poorly developed musculature and little body fat. Many years ago I went into the locked ward of a big psychiatric hospital and was shocked to see many of the patients looking very thin and gaunt. Since then I have often wondered why so few researchers and psychiatrists pay attention to this dramatic weight and muscle loss.

Dietary fads

Here is another mother's description of her son, very acutely observed:

> Extreme dietary fads – potatoes are evil! – vegetarianism, quantities of raw porridge oats eaten, great sporadic thirst, two to three pints of water drunk at a sitting, considerable weight loss, unable to get up some days, waxy pallor, hyperactivity towards evening/night. Unrealistic career ideas which changed every day. Continual sorting out of belongings/room. Making elaborate plans/lists for never-attempted unrealistic projects. Playing loud music on guitar or records. For a year I described these things every week to a senior child/adolescent psychologist. Finally persuaded son to see him. Prescribed tricyclics (like, for example, amitriptyline). Violent outbreak, *sectioned*, attempt on brother's life and £300 damage. ['Sectioned' is the term used when a patient is admitted to a psychiatric hospital under a numbered section of the Mental Health Act as written, i.e. Section 2.]

These last actions were probably caused by the tricyclics, the mother thought. I think she was quite right – this young man, who should have been given anti-schizophrenic medication, was prescribed a drug which only made his condition worse.

Difficulties with eating and jaw articulation

From her work with schizophrenic children Dr Sheila Cantor noted that a poor ability to chew in a three-year-old may emerge as an articulation defect later. One young adult schizophrenic whom I know was only able to open his mouth a very little way. He had been told by his psychiatrist that it was psychosomatic. Eventually the condition was operated on, and although he still could not open his mouth very wide it was better. The surgeon told him it was a genuine physical problem and not psychosomatic.

Other patients appear to have different eating problems. In a letter in the *American Journal of Psychiatry* (1986) about

27

swallowing style in adults, Dr Robert Keith said that after child-hood schizophrenics did not seem able to switch to a more mature way of swallowing: 'In the immature swallowing pattern the jaw muscles do not set, the tongue moves forward slightly and the lips slightly pout or pucker.' He reported that in an examination of twenty-five adult patients, all swallowed with the tongue-thrust style characteristic of young children, which may be a sign of abnormal brain development.

When we asked SAGB members if they had noticed any abnor-malities in swallowing, we received a number of interesting and helpful replies. One mother said:

> My daughter has always had a problem with a very loud clicking jaw when she eats any food at all. It makes a very loud noise when chewing food – most embarrassing if you have company. She has chronic paranoid schizophrenia. Her eldest sister also has a very noisy jaw – when eating it clicks – and my youngest daughter has had a problem with swallowing and thinking she's going to die since she was fifteen.

One patient wrote very helpfully about her swallowing problems:

> Sometimes I have to swallow three or so times before I can swallow the food. I have noticed this sort of silent struggle with a patient in the day centre with liquids from a cup or glass, especially cold water. I swallow and almost choke. My breathing is lost and I am really frightened that this will one day be the death of me. If I sip, then remove the glass and breathe, it is better, but if I continue swallowing to drink more than one gulp, I lose control and have to quickly remove the glass from my mouth to get my breath. It helps if I first take a deep breath, then breathe out, then drink while I breathe in. But if I go on drinking and breathing, I choke. The water would go down into my lungs.

Two mothers described their sons' eating problems. The first said: 'My son has difficulty in swallowing – he doesn't appear to masticate his food – and he puckers his lips when drinking. He had difficulty as a youngster, when he always appeared clumsy

28

in his eating method.' The second told us: 'My son frequently seems to swallow either too rapidly or with his mouth too full, which makes him cough and splutter and choke until he has cleared his throat. He never used to do this before the illness came on.' Another correspondent, writing on his own behalf, said: 'Also I do seem to do the tongue-thrust thing when I eat. I noticed a Mongol girl did it a few weeks ago in a restaurant, but much more pronounced than I do.' Surely every effort should be made to find out what relevance these eating problems have to the disease process.

Moving from difficulties associated with chewing and swallowing to those connected with food itself, here is another mother's description of the problems encountered by her son.

My son had to attend a child guidance clinic for bed-wetting from the ages of eight to eleven. Bad-tempered baby, suffered from asthma. Went to ordinary school but not a good scholar, work very untidy and didn't want to do hard work – though hyperactive physically. Neighbours told me he never spoke to them or noticed them, like his sisters did.

He had difficulty getting jobs when he left school because he had no qualifications, so he had to take jobs in bakeries. The jobs were all too much for him and he was always brought home sick.

Looking back, I see he was too sick to work. He looked half-dead from about eighteen, especially his eyes. I kept taking him to the doctor saying I didn't like the look of him, but the doctor said there was nothing wrong with him.

He became more solitary, just playing his electric guitar and obsessed with records. At twenty he had hallucinations and was diagnosed after a few days in hospital. Since then it has been seven years of misery and deterioration.

On reviewing his childhood I recall the bed-wetting started towards the end of his junior school days and into the first years of secondary school. No obvious explanations – e.g. new baby, death in family. No changes, in fact.

Again, this man seems to have been food-sensitive as a baby, since he suffered from asthma. The cause may have been sensitivity to milk. Despite the mother's plea for help for her son, the diagnosis was delayed until the arrival of hallucinations. The bed-wetting, untidy writing and hyperactivity may all have been aspects of the disease exhibited many years earlier.

This is another account of a schizophrenic who had probably always been food-sensitive:

> Our daughter had three months colic, then convulsions in her third year which had no obvious cause. She was not a cuddly baby, preferring to sit on the edge of my lap rather than snuggle up – a naturally dignified little girl with a queenly manner, not the usual rough-and-tumble child at play. Very stuffy nose and mucus problems at about six. Behaviour wonderful until ten or eleven, when suddenly became very demanding but would not toe family and household line over duties (only small ones asked of her). School work started going off until she became a very unhappy teenager – found it hard to make friends – diagnosed schizophrenic on leaving school at seventeen. Thought I was poisoning her. My daughter is wheat-allergic.

The colic and mucus problems of this girl may both have been related to food sensitivity, with milk perhaps causing the mucus problems (see p. 133).

Bowel disorders

The following childhood case history is described by another SAGB member, the brother of a patient who does not appear to be medicated.

> He started trouble with his bowels with bouts of the runs. A locum examined him in a children's hospital for possible signs of TB, but could find nothing. Not long after this our parents had to call in a doctor, who diagnosed measles, but it seems the form it had taken was unusual.
>
> Later he went to the infants' school, but he was only able to stay a week because of copious running of the bowel. The doctor then diagnosed colitis. He went through stages of the

complaint, during which time he had fits of short duration which subsequently cleared up.

He lost all traces of the colitis some twenty years ago (when he was twenty-three). Apart from incontinence with wetting, he now passes normal motions.

This member then goes on to talk about his brother's present condition. He does not mention any drug treatment, but says his brother suddenly goes white, his mind goes off at a tangent, and he starts talking about completely irrelevant things. 'For this I give him one or two doses of magnesium phosphate, after which he loses the symptoms completely.' This case history was interesting because of the bowel trouble at an early stage. The bed-wetting and the fits may be of importance, while the magnesium phosphate could well be of help to others with similar symptoms.

A shutter descending

This is a patient's own description of the onset of his illness:

Concentration was not so long-lasting for about one year before onset, though my work was satisfactory. Then one evening I had a vomit. Two or three days afterwards a shutter came down (this is the best way I can describe it) over my eyes; my brain mechanism went out of place and all my past life was confused. This occurred in a fraction of a second. In that moment I was completely changed as a personality.

Diametrically changed opinions

Here is another first-person account, by a woman, of the form her illness takes:

Loss of appetite, dramatic weight loss, nervous diarrhoea, a feeling of being poisoned, anxiety, insomnia (not relieved by sleeping pills), crying fits in the early stages.

Overactivity initially, followed by an inability to concentrate on radio, television or newspapers, afraid to answer phone or door. After approximately a week's sleeplessness becoming

31

totally disorientated as to time and place, with irrational thoughts and fears. Not eating or drinking.

The frightening aspect of the disease in my case is that I could be a perfectly happy, balanced, outgoing and motivated person one week, and yet ten days later be so irrational, unbalanced and confused that I had to be admitted to hospital. During bad phases I certainly experience a reversal of previously strongly held opinions and attitudes.

The reversal of strongly held ideas is quite common. For example, people change their political affiliation to the opposite of what they were previously, or become religious when they were agnostic before the onset of their illness.

Childhood illnesses

Here is one young man's early history as recounted by his father:

He was born healthy and normal. As a child he had mumps, measles, chicken pox and an internal staphylococcal infection. He started school at five and made friends without any difficulty, but did not work very hard. He was occasionally reprimanded for naughtiness but learnt easily. At ten or eleven he went round with friends who got into trouble, though he managed to avoid it himself. He also suffered from hay fever. At fifteen he had a cyst on his forehead, which was lanced in hospital. At seventeen he started drinking and smoking 'pot'. When he was twenty and we could no longer cope, we took him to see a psychiatrist who diagnosed schizophrenia after one day.

The most characteristic early symptoms here were the infections: the normal viral infections of mumps, measles and chicken pox, and the staphylococcal infection and the cyst on his head – although no mention was made of whether any organism was found in the cyst. The other aspect was that boy had hay fever. It would seem that the immune system was involved, and was perhaps not as efficient as it could have been.

The alcohol and 'pot' may just have been a natural part of growing up, but could equally have been taken to try to stave off the oncoming but as yet undiscovered illness. They usually make schizophrenia worse, but probably give an immediate feeling of well-being. One patient told me that when she took cannabis it made her thinking become as clear as it used to be. No doubt this did not have any long-lasting beneficial effect, but it was understandable that she had wanted to take it. Many schizophrenics have a history of taking street drugs and alcohol.

Fantasizing

Here is a patient's description of her schooldays:

> At school, teachers were asking new pupils if they had any older brothers and sisters. I had none. So I invented one, and in my daydreams I had this big brother who could do everything. So could I, as sportsman, doctor, scientist, musician, speaker of many languages. I would project myself out of the room into the English teacher's room and tell him of all the wonderful deeds I had done.

This girl was obviously fantasizing all the while, and could probably hardly distinguish between reality and fantasy.

Early symptoms rejected by psychiatrists

This mother's account is of a fourteen-year-old boy, the son of the man described in Chapter 1 whose driving changed according to his mood. Tragically, he also seems to be mentally ill. Even more tragically, despite the mother's efforts no one seems prepared to confirm this.

> My eldest child is violent, expects people to do what he wants them to, does not seem to understand when things are explained to him, does irrational things like throwing the cat out of the bedroom window during the night, and persuades his younger brother to accompany him under threat of a beating up. He kicks his sister whenever I go out of the room, and kicks me if I try to intervene between him and his brother, who is three and

a half years younger and small for his age. The madness goes on in my son – I have escaped the ordeal and cruel behaviour of my ex-husband, but I cannot escape my son.

The psychiatrist who is supposed to have assessed my son says, 'Your son is immature, and will get worse as he gets older. He will almost certainly have to finish his education in a residential school and cannot be expected ever to attend an ordinary school.'

I asked: 'Is my son schizophrenic?'

He answered: 'What do you know of schizophrenia?'

I said: 'Nothing.'

He said: 'I stress that your son is immature and unlikely to get better.'

I said that if my son was immature then surely as he got older he should rationalize.

'No,' he said, and stated he had done all he could for the boy. He could not keep him in the clinic any longer because his attitude to other children was so aggressive, and asked whether I could take him home until arrangements were made to take him into a residential school. He also stressed that he was dangerous to me and the rest of the family.

I asked if there was any medication that could be given him.

The answer was: 'Do you want him sitting in a corner, staring into space? There is nothing.'

There has always been something different about my eldest son. He bit other children in primary school, climbed on top of the kitchen table and screamed for hours for no reason, and told his teachers I beat him up (I did not, although I would smack him if he did wrong). He used to attack other children often, both in school and outside. He went to a total of three primary schools because he accused the teachers of picking on him and the children of ganging up on him. He said that I and his brother and sister hated him. I've had numerous parents and teachers complaining about his behaviour. The police are now involved because of an attack on his teacher. I find the future black, as there seems to be no help for him.

Is this schizophrenia?

Most certainly I think it is, and no one is helping this mother.

Summary of early schizophrenia symptoms

The picture of early schizophrenia which emerges from this small survey of members, some of whose experiences have been described above, contained a mix of physical and behavioural problems. There was evidence of:

- Exhaustion
- Inability to concentrate
- Poor body temperature control
- Pallor
- Extreme weight loss
- Feeding difficulties
- Colic
- Anorexia
- Susceptibility to sometimes severe viral and bacterial infections
- Susceptibility to allergies, including asthma
- Abnormal nervous control of muscles
- Abnormal strength
- Strange neck position
- Bed-wetting
- Very untidy work
- Hyperactivity
- Difficulty in pot training when infants
- Mouth pouting
- Restlessness
- Fits
- Aggression
- Promiscuity
- Bad temper
- Obsessive behaviour
- Secrecy
- Suspicion

Research in France and the USA

In a French study (1986) by two French doctors, M. Bourgeois and J. J. Etachepare, the parents of thirty-five adult schizophrenics were asked to look back, as SAGB members had been,

35

at their children's early symptoms. (The French study covered two periods, from birth to five years and from six to twelve years, whereas the SAGB members' accounts went on well into adolescence and young adulthood.) The parents of thirty-five normal children, used as 'controls', were also asked to remember any early difficulties or abnormalities in their children. Here is a summary of the results:

0–5 years

	Schizophrenics	Controls
Sleeping difficulties	15	8
Feeding difficulties	14	7
Lack of bladder control	12	2
Behavioural problems	14	5
Very good and docile children	11	2

6–12 years

	Schizophrenics	Controls
Withdrawal/isolation	17	1
Phobic/obsessional	12	5
Lack of bladder control	10	2
'Not with it'	8	1
Anxious	6	0
Bizarre behaviour/ideas	6	1
Excessive shyness	6	0

Childhood schizophrenia

Schizophrenia that begins in childhood – as opposed to early pre-disease symptoms of a condition that will later be identified as adult schizophrenia – can be extremely harmful, and young children who have the disease seem to forget the words they have already learnt.

A survey conducted in America on child schizophrenics up to the age of fifteen concluded that it affected far more boys than girls, whereas adult schizophrenia was more evenly distributed between the sexes. Dr Barbara Fish considers childhood schizophrenia to be continuous with adult schizophrenia. In child schizophrenics, she says,

> Language and cognition [knowing] were seriously affected in the first two years of life at the very beginning of the illness. . . . [It is] a biologically more severe form of the disease that primarily produces a greater disruption of central nervous system functioning . . . difficulty in walking was among the early developmental symptoms that significantly differentiated pre-schizophrenic children from the others.

The neurological symptoms included:

- Hypo-activity (reduced movement – as opposed to hyperactivity, which is excessive movement)
- Rigidity
- Abnormal walk
- Poor co-ordination
- Impaired attention

Dr Sheila Cantor's excellent book *The Schizophrenic Child* (1982) is extremely useful for all families with a history of mental illness. Dr Cantor says that someone whose illness has started in childhood shows typical adult schizophrenic symptoms when he reaches the age at which schizophrenia is usually diagnosed – adolescence or early adulthood. She says that

> when schizophrenia begins in childhood its effect upon normal development is devastating. Islands of normal or even gifted functions remain in a child who otherwise appears functionally retarded. Too often the behavioural and sleep disturbances which accompany the disease 'burn' out the family . . . resulting in the child being institutionalised.

Dr Cantor's most important finding is that in childhood schizo-phrenics the motor system is significantly impaired. Motor nerves are those which cause muscles to move.

In her description of schizophrenic babies she stresses how beautiful and fine-skinned the majority are, though a few are born floppy, with poor muscle tone and sucking ability. The baby may have a club foot, dislocated hips or crossed eyes. For the first year the schizophrenic infant may stick to a single activity, once begun – surely the beginning of obsessional behaviour in the adult. The baby may be awake a lot at night, and be difficult to feed as he eats so slowly. Speech is often tardy to develop. The toddler finds it very difficult to control his emotions, and may scream for hours in a temper tantrum. Every sound, smell and sight strikes this child with equal intensity. Poor muscle tone interferes with development, and a few children walk on their toes – characteristic also of some adult schizophrenics.

Summary of symptoms in very young children

According to Cantor the symptoms for which the parent seeks medical help are generally:

- 'Speech delay'
- The child's preoccupation with his own world
- Hyperactivity
- Doing the opposite of what he is asked
- Temper tantrums
- Isolation from other children

Other symptoms noted in the pre-school years are:

- The toddler taking what he wants from other children
- 'Mirthless' laughter
- Poor co-ordination of chewing and tongue movements
- Drooling
- Slowness of eating
- The child may, on the other hand, be very quick at puzzles and with mechanical objects

At three or four, the nursery school and kindergarten child may 'treat all individuals as if they were extensions of himself. He cannot comprehend that they may have ideas and wishes of their own.' He may carry out 'a single activity for an astonishingly long time. He may be hyperactive and indulge in aimless activity or stereotyped activity such as episodes of rapid pacing or jumping up and down on one spot – motor activity is notably jerky or clumsy.'

The highly functioning child with paranoid schizophrenia may develop persecutory or grandiose delusions and appear

strangely pre-occupied and intense for one so young. It is this child who is often a constant questioner with a very high anxiety level. His senses are extraordinarily alert. He may ask a lot of questions compulsively but at about seven or eight years he may begin to construct answers to his own questions based on faulty information. When he stops asking questions and begins inventing his own answers the paranoia begins.

On speech problems Dr Cantor says:

All schizophrenic children are thought disordered. About 50 per cent of schizophrenic children make up new words. Sometimes their speech is disorganised. They may echo what others say and may talk to themselves. Sometimes the child speaks very softly so he can barely be heard and in the next moment may speak in an astonishingly loud voice. The child seems to lack the ability to judge when he is speaking loudly or softly. The speech is precise and formal.

Summary of symptoms in older children

The main symptoms to watch for, according to Dr Cantor, are:

- Long hands
- Decreased muscle power and muscle mass
- Increased head circumference
- Prominent bridge of the nose
- Deep-set eyes
- Short fingers
- Lax elbows and wrist and finger joints
- Crossed eyes
- Articulation defects
- Flat feet

- No arm-swinging when walking
- Abnormal walk (on toes)
- Dilated eye pupils
- Pallor

Additionally, one survey revealed that a sample of schizophrenic patients were significantly smaller than a similar sample of normal people. They were smaller in height, chest circumference, chest expansion, hip circumference and width of the shoulders; and their bodies were altogether narrower.

If schizophrenia could be tentatively diagnosed when parents or other relations first report a marked personality change to the doctor, and then treated, a good response would be all that was needed to confirm the diagnosis. It would be far better than waiting for the severe symptoms of delusions, hallucination and marked thought disorder. I fervently wish psychiatrists would forget those meaningless interim diagnoses of personality disorder, psychopathic disorder and so on, and not give other names to a disease of such severity as schizophrenia.

References

BRODOFF, AMI S. (1988): *First Person Accounts*. Schizophrenia Bulletin Vol. 14, No. 1.

BOURGEOIS, M.; ETACHEPARE, J. J. (1986): *Les Schizophrenes avant la Schizophrenie*. Ann. Med. Psychol. (Paris) 144 (7) pp. 757-66.

CANTOR, S. (1982): *The Schizophrenic Child*. Montreal, Canada. Eden Press.

CLOUSTON, T. S. (1898): *Clinical Lectures*. In 'Mental Diseases'. London. J. & A. Churchill.

FISH, BARBARA (1977): *Antecedents of Schizophrenia in Children*. Arch. Gen. Psych. Vol. 43.

HENDERSON, D. K. & GILLESPIE, R. D. (1937): A Textbook of Psychiatry. Oxford Medical Publication.

KEITH, ROBERT (1986): *Swallowing in Schizophrenia*. The American Journal of Psychiatry. 143: 11.

3

THE POSSIBLE CAUSES

There is still considerable uncertainty about the nature of schizophrenia amongst the medical profession. The Schizophrenia Association of Great Britain was founded in 1970 on a belief that
schizophrenia is a genetically inherited disease in which the
chemistry of the brain becomes disturbed, leading to altered
behaviour, thought and emotion.

There are still, after almost twenty years, many doctors who
do not agree with us and who think the disease is caused by
environmental factors – psycho-social ones at that. In other
words, families are still being blamed for the production of the
disease.

The two major schools of thought

In a television programme in August 1988 Dr T. J. Crow, one of
the leading British researchers into the causes of schizophrenia,
drew attention to the dichotomy within the medical profession.
'We don't know all the causes,' he said. 'Genes may be contributory. Families do not cause schizophrenia.' Many experts
nowadays are sure it is a hereditary disease (though not all
members of a family are affected, and it can leave whole
generations untouched); I side with this view. Others, however, still cling to the previously held theory that the disease
is environmental – in other words, that it is circumstances
in one's upbringing and family life that bring on the condition, rather than an inherited propensity to be schizophrenic.

41

The case for heredity

In *An Anatomy of Melancholy* (1652) Burton was quite familiar with the idea of madness as an inherited disease. He quoted an even earlier physician named Hector Boethius, who wrote of the harsh and dreadful measures taken by primitive societies to prevent madness – and other diseases which we now know not to be hereditary – being passed down to future generations:

> Heretofore in Scotland if any were visited with the falling disease [epilepsy], madness, gout, leprosy or any such dangerous disease, which was likely to be propagated from the father to the son, he was instantly gelded; a woman kept from all company of men and if by chance having some such disease, she was found to be with child, she with her brood were buried alive and this was done for the common good lest the whole nation should be injured or corrupted.

Fear was the prevailing emotion here, and one can see how the stigma attached to schizophrenia – which still exists today – arose in the first place.

Burton also quoted the views of the Spanish physician Lodovicus Mercatus: 'And madness after a set time comes to many which he calls a miraculous thing in nature and sticks forever to them as an incurable habit. And that which is more to be wondered at, it skips in some families the father and goes to the son, or takes every third in a lineal descent and doth not always produce the same but some like and a symbolising disease.'

Members of the SAGB with a schizophrenic son or daughter frequently confirm this when they say they can find no evidence of the disease elsewhere in their family – but then remark that an uncle was alcoholic, or a great-aunt was depressed and nervy. Dr Hugh Gurling's (1988) researches at the Middlesex Hospital Medical School in London provide evidence for this connection. He has found that schizophrenic members of a small number of families have a gene that is also carried by other family members who suffer from alcoholism, phobic disorder, depression and so on. These last are the 'symbolising diseases' of Lodovicus Mercatus; they are not schizophrenia, to be sure, but they are sufficiently similar to be included in the same spectrum. The race is now on among molecular geneticists to find the relevant gene: at least four research teams around the world are devoting their energies to this vital task.

Abortion or medication?

When the position of the gene(s) has been found on a particular chromosome then the chemical for which it codes has to be identified. It may turn out to be an enzyme or a receptor. When it is discovered it should lead to the development of rational treatments. This, of course, was not the way the current anti-schizophrenic medications were discovered. The drug Largactil (chlorpromazine) was being developed as an anti-histamine drug when, quite accidentally, it was found to have anti-psychotic, anti-schizophrenic properties. When the researchers find out what the actual genetic error – the faulty chemical – is, in schizophrenia, then they will be able to develop treatments in the real expectation that they will work. Serendipity will not be needed. Schizophrenia could become a conquered disease in a few years' time. If it is found to be a disease similar to phenylketonuria, and I think it will, then the treatment may well turn out to be a dietary one started at birth. Alternatively treatment could be started at the first sign of symptoms in someone found to have the faulty gene.

We have no need to be afraid of a disease when it is controllable and yet I notice in recent newspaper reports of genetic studies in schizophrenia that once the gene is identified, mothers carrying a baby (foetus) with the gene could have an abortion on these grounds, behaviour surely reminiscent of the happenings Hector Boethius described in the dark days. In one of the Scandinavian countries it is already possible for a schizophrenic mother to have an abortion on the grounds of her schizophrenia. The abortion of foetuses carrying the gene would go one step further. Schizophrenics and their families are amongst the most creative people. It would be tragic if all our future geniuses were aborted. A controlled schizophrenia is surely what we need; creativity without sickness – that must be our aim and not the facile solution of abortion.

The environmentalists

Not long ago I received a tragic letter from an SAGB member about a friend who for twenty years had visited her schizophrenic daughter in hospital daily. Then she was told by the staff to visit less frequently, because, they said, it was her upbringing of the girl which had caused the problem in the first place. After twenty years of devotion and care it was too much for the mother, who committed suicide.

The people who so distressed this woman belonged to the group known as environmentalists, who are convinced that schizophrenia is largely caused by psycho-social factors. Their beliefs are summed up in these words from a paper distributed by a fringe group in connection with the 1988 Conservative Party Conference:

> Mental illness is not catching, neither is it hereditary, although people are more likely to be affected if they grow up in a family where parents are unable to show affection or give positive guidance. Many factors in today's world put people under considerable stress. Poverty, unemployment, poor housing conditions are facts of twentieth-century life. Personality plays a part as well. People who are particularly sensitive and emotional may be much more vulnerable to stress. In most cases, mental illness is the result of a combination of factors.

Once the faulty gene is tracked down, ideas like this may have to be thrown out of the window. However, there may still be grounds for argument. . . .

Where heredity and environment join battle

While molecular geneticists are full of excitement and hope, as are the patients and their families, the environmentalists still have a card to play. They point out that, if schizophrenia *is* inherited, as their opponents claim, it does not follow the strict laws of genetics.

Genes were identified by the nineteenth-century Austrian scientist Gregor Mendel as being either dominant or recessive. A dominant gene, such as the one causing Huntington's chorea, for example, never skips a generation. Each child of an affected parent has a 50 per cent chance of inheriting the gene, and everyone who does inherit it will get the disease. A recessive gene, on the other hand, will tend to be suppressed by a dominant one. Someone will only exhibit the effects of a recessive gene if they receive the same recessive gene from each parent. If, however, the recessive gene is on the X sex chromosome a father cannot give it to his son, but a mother who is a carrier of the gene can do so. This chromosome is a probable candidate for the faulty gene in at least one sub-group of schizophrenics. The gene may or may not be recessive. I suspect it may. This is the mode of transmission in which I personally am most interested.

If the gene for schizophrenia is a dominant one, as is currently thought by some researchers, it may be that its effect is reduced in some people by other genes, which, according to Dr Ming T. Tsuang (1980), 'might chemically blockade the schizophrenia gene when present in the right strength of combinations'. Leonard L. Heston wrote in 1973 about schizoid behaviour (exhibiting the milder symptoms of schizophrenia, such as social withdrawal and eccentricity) amongst relatives of schizophrenics:

> Among males, anti-social behaviour has been found commonly enough to warrant the older sub-designation 'schizoid psychopath' . . . impulsive seemingly illogical crime such as arson, unreasoning assault and poorly planned theft. Social isolation, heavy intake of alcohol and sexual deviance have been noted frequently. Other schizoids, both male and female, have been described as eccentric, suspicion-ridden recluses. . . . Rigidity of thinking, blunting of affect [little response to their own emotions], anhedonia [inability to experience pleasure], exquisite sensitivity, suspiciousness and a relative poverty of ideas – in variable combinations and intensities – characterise both the schizoid and the schizophrenic. Though schizoids do not show a well-marked thought disorder, delusions and hallucinations, descriptions of some of the behavioural lapses of schizoids . . . are bizarre enough to suggest micro-psychotic episodes.

Other experts who subscribe to the 'dominant gene' theory have suggested something slightly different – that because of incomplete penetration, in a percentage of cases the *effects* of the disease are concealed.

Yet other researchers believe that it is a recessive gene on an autosomal and not a sex chromosome that is responsible for schizophrenia – in other words, it would need to be inherited from both parents. One study showed that if both parents were schizophrenic 82 per cent of their children suffered mental illness (with over 50 per cent it was actual schizophrenia). From my own experience I know that, for instance, the mother of a schizophrenic child may perhaps suffer from a mild depression or anxiety, whereas the father may be quick-tempered or slightly manic. Neither parent would be considered to have schizophrenia, yet the disposition away from normality can be seen to be there.

The genetic risk to relatives

Various studies have been carried out over the past twenty years or so to support the genetic theory. One of them used over a thousand pairs of twins, and concluded that if one twin had schizophrenia there was a much greater risk of the second twin developing the disease if the twins were identical (in other words, had identical genes) rather than non-identical. The fact that not all the second twins contracted the disease – only 86 per cent – implies that the remaining 14 per cent must have been prevented from doing so by environmental factors.

In *Genes and the Mind* Dr Ming Tsuang gives the following table of risks. He kindly allowed me to reproduce the table.

Risks to relatives of schizophrenics*

Relation	Risk (%)
First-degree relatives:	
Parents	4.4
Brothers and sisters	8.5
neither parent schizophrenic	8.2
one parent schizophrenic	13.8
Fraternal twin, opposite sex**	5.6
same sex**	12.0
Identical twin**	57.7
Children	12.3
both parents schizophrenic	36.6

Second-degree relatives:

Uncles and aunts	2.0
Nephews and nieces	2.2
Grandchildren	2.8
Half-brothers/sisters	3.2

First cousins (third-degree relatives)	2.9

General population	0.86

* Unless otherwise noted, figures are based on Slater and Cowie (1971); data mainly derived from pooled data of Zerbin-Rudin (1967), with only cases of definite schizophrenia counted.
** Pooled data based on Shields and Slater (1967)

In this table, too, only a certain percentage of identical twins both have schizophrenia. The environmentalists could say that the disease was in part caused by genes and in part by upbringing. Certainly it would be expected that if schizophrenia were totally genetic then both identical twins should always get the disease if one did. We in the Schizophrenia Association of Great Britain believe that more acceptable environmental factors could be diet or infection, or a combination of these. It is however only the psychological and social causes that the environmentalists consider.

L. L. Heston (1966) approached the hereditary/environment problem in a different way. He examined forty-seven adopted children whose mothers were schizophrenic and compared them with fifty adopted children – 'controls' – whose mothers were not schizophrenic. He found that the same percentage of children of schizophrenic mothers developed the disease as would have been expected to if they had been brought up in their own homes: 11 per cent, as opposed to 0 per cent of the controls. He also discovered that 28 per cent had a neurotic personality compared with 14 per cent of the controls; additionally, 9 per cent had mental deficiency compared with 0 per cent of the controls. To sum up, in Heston's study 67 per cent of the adopted-away children of schizophrenic mothers were not normal, compared with 18 per cent of the controls, proving beyond doubt the importance of genetic factors.

The American Dr S. Kety, doing a similar study in reverse, came to the same conclusion. He investigated the families of thirty-three people who were schizophrenic and had been adopted away from them as babies. The controls were thirty-three normal adopted people. Dr Kety found that 21 per cent of the relatives of the schizophrenics had schizophrenia or similar psychiatric conditions, whilst only 11 per cent of the relatives of the controls suffered in this way.

Despite the fact that both these studies confirmed the strong genetic component in schizophrenia, they did not identify it as the sole component. Thus they showed a strong genetic component but there *were* grounds for the environmentalists to say environment – meaning family, mother, society, etc. – was contributing to the disease. If they had thought of environment in terms of diet or infection instead of allocating blame they would surely have been closer to the truth.

A disease of the gut, not of the brain?

Let us consider phenylketonuria, a disease which can cause mental retardation. This is a recessively inherited disease in which the genetically caused faulty chemistry is known. The genetic defect codes for an enzyme, phenylalanine hydroxylase, which converts the amino-acid phenylalanine into tyrosine. The treatment is a dietary one and at birth, if the baby is found to have the disease, the amino-acid phenylalanine is kept very low (as it is an essential amino-acid it cannot be entirely excluded) and mental retardation is thus prevented. Here therefore is a genetically inherited disease in which the chief environmental factor causing the symptomology is the food eaten.

Perhaps a disease even more similar to schizophrenia is homocystinuria because it has similar psychotic symptoms. Dr. Derek Richter cited the case of a young man of twenty-one with a history of schizophrenia of nine years' duration. He was investigated and found to be excreting large quantities of homocystine in his urine. Because of this he was re-diagnosed as suffering not from schizophrenia, but from homocystinuria, a genetically determined enzyme defect which decreases the ability of the body to metabolise the amino-acid methionine, a constituent of most protein. This patient was again given dietary treatment and put on a low methionine diet. The parents had previously been blamed for his illness.

'Diet is the mother of diseases,' wrote Burton. 'Let the father be what he will, and from this alone melancholy and frequent other maladies arise.' Burton also said that a person will become mentally ill if he is 'born of a depressed mother and a bad diet together'. I think he was right and that a combination of a faulty gene and a diet incompatible with this gene will produce schizophrenia. I think schizophrenia will eventually be controlled through a dietary treatment, perhaps initiated at birth, for those with the faulty gene. I am sure we should be thinking in terms of diet as producing disease in those with the gene for schizophrenia, rather than seeing mother as the witch who makes her child ill.

Professor Lennart Wetterberg of the Karolinska Institute in Sweden described his studies at conferences organised by the Schizophrenia Association of Great Britain in 1978 and 1982. He was examining a population of six thousand people who went to Northern Sweden about 350 years ago. In one of three large pedigrees there are now over two hundred schizophrenics and the last three generations have been examined for enzyme and hormonal abnormalities. Professor Wetterberg concludes: 'Knowing that steroids are important regulators of enzyme activities the mechanisms by which the hormones affect the catecholamine-related enzymes in humans and particularly in schizophrenic patients merit high priority attention.' The neuro-transmitters dopamine, noradrenaline and adrenaline are catecholamines. It seems highly possible that the genetic fault in schizophrenia may prove to be an enzyme on the metabolic pathway which converts the amino acid tyrosine, via dopamine, to adrenaline. Tyrosine can derive from the protein in our diet or can be made in the body from the amino acid phenylalanine which itself *can* only be derived from dietary protein. In the USA, Professor Richard H. Wurtman of the Massachusetts Institute of Technology says that food directly affects the brain and that

the brain components that most markedly exhibit the effect of nutrition are the neurotransmitters [for example dopamine, shortage of which can cause Parkinson's disease]. . . . It ought to be possible for the physician to design diets that will have the

49

desired effect on the neurotransmitters. It should be possible to determine if the effects of particular diets on schizophrenics can be explained in biochemical terms by analysing their effects on brain neurotransmitters. . . .

Professor Henri Baruk, the distinguished French psychiatrist, agrees with these general hypotheses. In 1978 he wrote: 'It is not necessary to believe that the origin of mental illness is always in the brain, but that very often, on the contrary, the cause is very far from the brain, and the brain is only functionally disturbed by the toxins coming from the abdominal organs.' The trouble arises, he believes, where the hepatic vein (from the liver) meets the intestine; he suggests that many psychoses are determined by toxins from the digestive tract, and thinks a brain toxin produced by bacillus coli is formed in the gut and develops in the urinary tract – he cured a case of schizophrenia of twenty-five years' standing by using an anti-toxin to bacillus coli. Some ten years earlier Dr Hoenig (1967) had written that 'cardio-vascular renal [kidney] disease . . . has been found to occur more frequently amongst schizophrenics than in the general population'.

In 1978 Professor G. A. Buscaino, Professor of Psychiatry at the University of Naples, described the findings of his father, also a psychiatrist. As early as 1923 Professor Buscaino senior had begun to study the intestines of deceased schizophrenics and found: 'Five cases of congestion of the mucosa in spots and also haemorrhaging was noted in the small intestine and in one case even diffused patchy areas of atrophy.' By 1933, out of eighty-two schizophrenic patients autopsied gastritis had been reported in 50 per cent, enteritis in 88 per cent and colitis in 92 per cent. He subsequently found alteration in the liver of 83 per cent of 207 patients examined. Buscaino also received many reports on the abnormality of the bacteria and other organisms in the gut of these patients.

The American researcher Dr F. Curtis Dohan, writing in 1978, suggested a similarity between schizophrenia and coeliac disease. The damaged condition of the gut noted by Buscaino resembles that found in coeliac disease, where the villi – (tiny finger-like projections on the walls of the intestine through whose surface nutrients are absorbed into the blood) are damaged then flattened by wheat proteins, so that a condition of malabsorption arises.

Many nutrients may pass through the gut and be excreted rather than absorbed and possibly because of the gut damage, infectious organisms, bacteria, viruses and fungi could more readily gain access to the body and brain. It certainly seems possible that the same thing may happen for at least a sub-group of schizophrenics. There is as we know often weight loss and an increased susceptibility to infections. I do not know if patients with coeliac disease are prone to infections.

Infections – cause and effect

Infections can most certainly produce psychiatric symptoms. Appendicitis, for example, or kidney infections can cause mental symptoms. Earlier this century there was a high death rate from infections amongst schizophrenics, particularly from tuberculosis. It was said later that this was because of conditions in hospital which led to the disease being rife. It seems to me that other factors were involved. Nowadays there are much better preventative measures for tuberculosis. There is, however, a continuing high incidence of infections amongst schizophrenics and this should, I think, receive serious attention. We will see later that currently a virus causation is being suggested for schizophrenia.

Back in the seventeenth century Burton recognized that many diseases seemed to concentrate themselves in families where there was madness. A survey of SAGB members revealed a high incidence of certain other diseases in families with a schizophrenic member. Based on a sample of over three hundred families, the results were tabulated like this:

Constellation of diseases which may accompany schizophrenia in patients and close family members

Illness or complaint	in the subject	in relative(s) of the subject
Pernicious anaemia	5	22
Parkinson's disease	5	33
Addison's disease	0	1
Epilepsy	17	31
Multiple sclerosis	0	11
Thyroid disease	10	38

Coeliac disease	8	13
Diabetes	6	50
Peptic ulcer	3	26
Cancer of the stomach	0	33
Rheumatoid arthritis	9	74
Circulation problems	59	87
Kidney problems	11	24
Skin rashes	88	76
Joint pain	58	81
Fever	23	4
Water retention	31	34
Thirst	115	14
Muscle pain	61	45
Migraine	43	97
Swelling of face/neck	23	10

Family members undoubtedly outnumber the schizophrenics although the actual numbers are unknown.

The Schizophrenia Association of Great Britain asked its members about the incidence of coeliac disease in their families as they already had a schizophrenic member. The incidence of coeliac disease was very high, 8/340 amongst the schizophrenics and 13/340 in their near relatives. The incidence is 1/2000 in the general population. In 1985 Professor Bengt Jansson and his colleagues reported on a schizophrenic patient who did not respond to neuroleptic drugs. He did a bowel biopsy and found a coeliac condition, and when the patient was put on a grain-free diet he lost his psychosis. Dr D. N. Vlissides and his colleagues in Sheffield University put twenty-two very disturbed patients (whatever their diagnosis) in a closed ward in Rampton onto a grain-free diet. They all improved to some degree and two dramatically so, so that one was able to help on the ward rounds. Professor C. H. Mindham (1987) did a permeability study to see if there was a coeliac condition in schizophrenia. They did not find one but they did find abnormal gut permeability.

In both the Sheffield and Leeds experiments the patients were receiving neuroleptic medication at the same time as their gluten-free diet, which must have had an effect on the results. Similar work currently being undertaken at Bangor University, supported by the SAGB, includes investigations on the effects of neuroleptics on gut permeability. Without this knowledge the results of all future studies will be suspect.

Neuroleptics and the dopamine hypothesis

According to Canadian researcher Dr Alan Boulton, reporting on a conference held in Berlin in 1987, one speaker said that if everything about schizophrenia were put into a pot it would boil down to three things. The first, that the illness seems to run in families and therefore has a genetic component, has already been discussed. The second was that anti-psychotic drugs (neuroleptics) tend to help the symptoms, and the third that schizophrenic brains may have some structural abnormalities.

The second point, the fact that anti-psychotic drugs tend to ameliorate the symptoms, has been the departure point for much current research in schizophrenia. The dopamine hypothesis arose because patients given neuroleptic drugs often suffer from side-effects similar to the symptoms of Parkinson's disease – twitching, uncontrollable muscles, sometimes leading to impaired speech. These distressing symptoms are caused by a loss of neurones (nerve cells) containing the neurotransmitter called dopamine. The conclusion drawn from this is that in schizophrenia neuroleptics act by blocking dopamine receptors producing Parkinsonian side-effects. Thus, the argument goes, if neuroleptics reduce the amount of dopamine available, schizophrenia may be partly due to over-active dopamine transmission in the brain.

Another line of evidence is that amphetamines can induce schizophrenia-like symptoms and increase the release of dopamine. They can also precipitate a severe schizophrenic illness in someone with genetic vulnerability to the disease. The effects of amphetamine psychosis can be reversed by neuroleptic drugs. For all these reasons, the dopamine hypothesis is the most widely investigated hypothesis for the chemical basis of schizophrenia.

The action of neuroleptics on membranes

The discovery of neuroleptics has led, reasonably enough, to a concentration of research in the area of brain dopamine. But their action on dopamine receptors in the brain cannot by any stretch of the imagination be their only action on the body. The chemistry of both body and brain must be widely altered by these powerful drugs.

It seems to me that since a number of neuroleptic drugs stabilize membranes, including gut membranes, when given at a certain concentration, they might be exerting their chief beneficial action at this site rather than in the brain. Perhaps in unmedicated patients faulty metabolites (broken down products of digestion) are able to pass readily through a damaged gut into the bloodstream and thus adversely affect the brain chemistry. If medication then stabilized the gut membrane, such faulty metabolites could no longer reach the brain. P. Guth, one of the first to undertake research into the membrane-stabilizing effects of the drug chlorpromazine, wrote to me saying that it seemed to him and his colleagues that chlorpromazine might inhibit its own absorption, and that it would not be surprising if neuroleptics were found to inhibit gut permeability.

Two additional factors detract from the dopamine hypothesis. The first is that neuroleptics must be taken for a while before they become effective. Researchers working on the brain have found that when radioactively labelled medication reaches the brain and blocks the dopamine receptors, the clinical improvement does not take place immediately.

The second fact needing explanation is that a relapse does not occur for some while if the drug is withdrawn. It takes about three months for the symptoms to reassert themselves. Does it take this long for foods to start damaging the gut and starting the whole process over again? Maybe therefore it is not the direct action of the drug on the dopamine receptors which improves the schizophrenia but rather the action of the drug on the gut. Additionally blood levels of medication give no indication of therapeutic effect. Blood levels may be high and yet the patient does not get better. Membranes are not stabilised if the drug is at too high or too low a concentration. Drug blood levels have often been measured in order to see if enough medication is being given, but high blood levels do not necessarily produce good therapeutic response. Anti-schizophrenic medications like Largactil are now being given to treat diarrhoeal conditions because they prevent dehydration by preventing loss of fluid through the gut wall. We know therefore that they *do* have a major effect on the gut.

Structural changes in schizophrenic brains

The third point reported by Dr Alan Boulton concerned structural changes in the brains of some schizophrenia patients, as detected by scanners. Causes for the cerebral changes have been sought in damage at birth, or in exposure during pregnancy to infections which might have damaged the foetus's developing brain. The results of one study suggests that 'the cerebral changes seen in schizophrenia are non-progressive and probably ante-date the illness'. This conclusion is corroborated by other researchers, who also note that the abnormalities are not limited to schizophrenia patients but are seen additionally in those suffering from alcoholism, mental handicap and senile dementia. The 'enlarged brain ventricle' theory, therefore, may be no more than a red herring – if currently a very popular one.

The role of viruses

Research has also been carried out into the possibility of viruses, such as herpes and cytomegalovirus, having an effect on the developing brain. A Medical Research Council booklet entitled *Research into Schizophrenia*, published in 1987, suggested that 'a genetic predisposition to a virus which becomes latent [like the herpes virus] could explain some of the anomalies of familial occurrence, episodes of illness and seasonality of onset [an excess of winter over summer births in a proportion of schizophrenics has been found]'. It did not make any more positive conclusions, and nothing further has been found to support the idea of viral infection before birth.

It seems far more likely to me that infectious agents exacerbate or precipitate schizophrenia as the disease develops – due, as I have suggested, to a damaged gut mucosa. Most bacterial infections can now be dealt with very effectively by a wide range of antibiotics, and vaccines are available to deal with many viral infections. Fewer schizophrenics die today from infections, but even now viral infections such as influenza, measles and glandular fever seem regularly to push patients over into a schizophrenic breakdown if they are genetically vulnerable to the disease. It is not known why some people succumb more readily than others to infections, but perhaps the nutritional status and the wholeness of the membranes, especially those of the gut, are the most important factors.

There are no specific vaccines for schizophrenia, and antibiotics are not used as a treatment. Nevertheless, a course of penicillin given for a concurrent infection, whether or not it is known to be bacterial, has been found to improve the symptoms of schizophrenics. Strangely, also, an antibiotic has been found to improve the mental state of patients in the absence of any noticeable infection. It would be interesting to see the results of widespread trials of antibiotics as a short-term treatment for schizophrenia. I have already mentioned that Baruk treated a schizophrenic successfully with an anti-toxin to bacillus coli in the 1930s; the symptoms did not recur, and the patient went on to become a successful banker. We should not dismiss too readily the idea that micro-organisms may produce schizophrenic symptoms in some people – though perhaps only in the presence of damaged gut and other membranes.

Body and brain – a holistic view

So what is the nature of the beast? Is it:

● An infectious disease caused by an infection in the womb?
● The result of a retrovirus which has inserted itself into the genes?
● A chronic disease like cancer, but confined in its pathology to the brain?
● A chronic, inherited disease in which the entire body chemistry including the brain is affected?
● Or even, as some people still think, not a disease at all, in the usual sense of the word, but a condition caused by adverse psychological or sociological experiences?

If I had to stress one point over all others, it would be that the brain is inherently no different from the rest of the body. It is not a mysterious and isolated part of each human being. On the contrary, the connections between body and brain are very close, and the brain is but one organ of the body. The well body is in harmony with its well brain; if one suffers, the other will also. They are part of a single organism, and must not be considered separately.

There are also very close links between the digestive system and the brain. If we were able to understand how our diet affects our thoughts, emotions and behaviour we would take more care about what we eat – and think more clearly as a result (see Chapter 7).

The need for exhaustive research

Several years ago I saw a television documentary about a certain small district of China which had a very high incidence of cancer of the oesophagus – that part of the digestive tract between the mouth and the stomach. The Chinese were determined to find the cause, and, though they had few resources, investigated the disease with commendable thoroughness. They examined food, water and soil, and considered every other condition that might have been a contributory factor, but without success. Recently I met a Chinese psychiatrist working in the USA, who told me the end of the story. The cause of the cancer had been discovered to be fermented cabbage – a Chinese version of sauerkraut – in the fermentation of which a particular organism, apparently carcinogenic, had been used. The recipe had been brought from a region in the north of the country – which also suffered a high rate of oesophagal cancer.

This is the sort of intensive search which should be undertaken for the causes of schizophrenia. The disease has many facets, and there are already many pointers to the causes. We should use every shred of information now available and see if we can put the jigsaw together. It is interesting, in the light of the Chinese anecdote, that while schizophrenics have a lower incidence of lung cancer than the general population – despite the fact that many of them are very heavy smokers – they, too, have a higher-than-average rate of oesophagal cancer. That might be a very useful starting point.

I am very grateful to Professor Lennart Wetterberg, Head of the Department of Psychiatry in the famous Karolinska Institute in Sweden, for sending me part of his chapter for a new book to be published in the Spring of 1989 called *The Future of Genetics in Neuropsychiatry*. In this chapter Professor Wetterberg describes how very new and ever more complicated techniques are being developed to characterise the human genome (the complete set of genes on the chromosomes) and says that the new information obtained 'is likely to propel the genetic studies and bring psychiatry into the mainstream of modern molecular biology'. Of course, this optimism caused by the rapid progress in genetic research is entirely justified and enormously exciting. We are about to enter into another era of mankind when we will get to know ourselves very intimately through a knowledge of our genetic make-up.

Professor Wetterberg writes of the recent work by Hugh Gurling (Sherrington et al 1988) and of his own work (Kennedy et al 1988). Both groups reported in the same issue of 'Nature'. Wetterberg said that Sherrington reported on 'a genetic linkage to two DNA polymorphisms on the long arm of chromosome 5, found in members in five Icelandic and two British families, in which schizophrenia was frequent. In total, 104 family members, including 39 schizophrenic patients, were studied.' The gene itself is not yet identified. In the persons who showed linkage on chromosome 5 there were also cases of other mental disturbances not classified as nuclear schizophrenia.'

Wetterberg continued by saying that Kennedy et al reported on a 'study in a Swedish family complex including 81 members, 31 of whom had schizophrenia. The authors used eight DNA probes on chromosome 5 and found no linkage to schizophrenia, clearly indicating that schizophrenia may be caused by a gene defect other than that of chromosome 5.' Thus, Wetterberg concludes that such studies may 'help to break down schizophrenia into diagnostic sub-groups''.

As we considered earlier, the symptoms by which schizophrenia is diagnosed probably do not tell us about the real nature of the disease or diseases. We have seen that many disease conditions are already known to share the mental symptoms of schizophrenia. By getting down to the actual genetic errors we may find 'schizophrenia' constitutes many different disease conditions. The future looks very bright for schizophrenia and the new techniques will bring the solutions we long for probably more rapidly than any of us have yet dared hope.

References

BARUK, H., 'Psychoses from digestive origins' in *Biological Basis of Schizophrenia* (eds Hemmings, W. A. and Hemmings, Gwynneth). MTP Press, Lancaster, 1978.

BUSCAINO, G. A., 'The amino-hepatho-entero-toxic theory of schizophrenia: an historical evaluation' in *Biological Basis of Schizophrenia* (eds Hemmings, W. A. and Hemmings, Gwynneth). MTP Press, Lancaster, 1978.

DOHAN, F. Curtis, 'Schizophrenia: Are some food-derived polypeptides pathogenic? Coeliac disease as a model' in *Biological Basis of Schizophrenia* (eds Hemmings, W. A. and Hemmings, Gwynneth). MTP Press, Lancaster, 1978.

HESTON, L. L., 'Psychiatric disorders in foster home-reared children of schizophrenic mothers' in *British Journal of Psychiatry*, 112, 819–25, 1966.

HESTON, L. L., 'The genetics of schizophrenia and schizoid disease', in *Orthomolecular Psychiatry* (eds Hawkins and Pauling). Freeman, San Francisco, 1973.

HOENIG, J., *Recent Developments in Schizophrenia*. Royal Medico Psychological Association, Headley, 1967.

JANSSEN, B., KRISTJANSSON and NILSSON, 'Schizophrenic psychotic picture decreased in patient given gluten-free diet' in *Lakartidningen*, 81 (6), 448, 1984.

KENNEDY, J., GIUFFRAT, L. A., MOISES, Hans W., CAVALLI-SFORZA, L. L., PAKSTIS, A. J., KIDD, J. R., CASTIGLIONI, C. H., SJOGREN, B., WETTERBERG, Lennart, KIDD, K. K. (1988): 'Evidence against linkage of schizophrenia to markers on chromosome 5 in a Northern Swedish pedigree'. Nature (London) 336, 167–70.

KETY, S. S. and JACOBSEN, B., in *Genetic Research in Psychiatry* (eds Fieve, R. R., Rosenthal, D. and Brill, H., Johns Hopkins University Press, Baltimore, 1975.

SHERRINGTON, R., BRYNJOLFSSON, J., PETURSSON, H., POTTER, Mark, DUDDLESTON, K., BARRACLOUGH,

B., WASMUTH, J., DOBBS, M., GURLING, Hugh. (1988): 'Localisation of a susceptibility locus for schizophrenia on chromosome 5.' Nature (London) 336, 164–7.

SLATER, ELIOT, *Clinical Psychiatry*, Ballière, Tindal and Cassell, London, 1922.

TSUANG, M. T. and VANDERMEY, R., *Genes and the Mind*. OUP, New York, 1980.

VLISSADES, D. N., JENNER, E. and VENULET, A., 'A double blind gluten-free/gluten load controlled trial in a secure ward population', in *Brit. J. Psychol.*, 148, 447, 1980.

WETTERBERG, L., 'Clinical and biochemical manifestations of acute intermittent porphyria; a working model for schizophrenia as an inborn error of metabolism' in *Biological Basis of Schizophrenia* (eds Hemmings, W. A. and Hemmings, Gwynneth). MTP Press, Lancaster, 1978.

WETTERBERG, L., 'The genetic controls of catecholimines and its possible implication in schizophrenia' in *Biological Aspects of Schizophrenia and Addiction* (eds Hemmings, W. A. and Hemmings, Gwynneth). MTP Press, Lancaster, 1982.

WETTERBERG, L., 'The Future of Genetics in Neuropsychiatry'. In L. Wetterberg (ed.) *Genetics of Neuropsychiatric Diseases*. London, Macmillan Press. Wenner-Gren Center International Symposium Series. Vol. 51, 1989.

WURTMAN, R. J., 'The effect of diet on brain neurotransmitters' in *Biological Basis of Schizophrenia* (eds Hemmings, W. A. and Hemmings, Gwynneth). MTP Press, Lancaster, 1978.

4

MEDICAL TREATMENTS

'I feel as if a new life has been given me with the Priadel and Piportil,' a forty-year-old woman wrote to me not long ago. 'I would say to a person who is afraid of people, afraid someone is trying to kill them – try Priadel. It has made a new woman of me.' Up until that time she had been prescribed a number of different drugs, none of which had made her any better. At last a doctor had discovered the right drugs and the correct dosage for this particular patient – who was understandably overjoyed.

Realization of illness by patient is rare

That woman was a co-operative patient: she took the prescribed drugs and eventually got better. What, though, of the unco-operative young – usually male – paranoid schizophrenic, whose brain chemistry and personality have changed, and who may be violent in word and deed? How can he be helped? When he shouts at his family, blames them for every minor thing that goes wrong or that he imagines has gone wrong; when he thinks everyone around him has turned against him; when he is angry without cause, how can we help him? It is no use having the best drugs in the world if the patient refuses to believe he is mentally ill and feels grossly insulted if this is suggested to him.

This is perhaps the most terrible problem there is to be faced. It is impossible to persuade an angry, irrational patient to take medication he does not believe he needs. Everyone, including the doctor and social worker, is afraid of the paranoid patient. Undoubtedly the patient feels that fear and reacts to it, thus exacerbating an already difficult situation.

61

If untreated patients can acknowledge the fact that anger, violence, ceaseless criticism of others and feelings of persecution are disease symptoms, they will be halfway to helping themselves get well. They should try to understand that those whom they love are frightened when anger and blame are directed at them. Their families may shout back at them – then blazing rows erupt from which all parties find it difficult to extricate themselves. Everyone wants to be liked and loved, and to like and love in return. If untreated patients shout too much everyone *will* run away from them – their feelings of persecution will become self-fulfilling prophecies and they *will* be deserted. A person may not be mad, hallucinated, deluded or incoherent in his speech, but if his emotions run away *with* him others will run away *from* him.

Try this test. Whenever you believe you have cause to be angry, pause a moment and ask yourself: 'Can I stop myself from being angry? Might it be better to stay calm in the face of what I imagine is deliberate provocation?' If you think the answer to the second question is 'Yes', and yet you constantly find yourself unable to stop arguing angrily, then you need help. Medication can and does get rid of irrational anger and paranoia. Remember, the symptoms that need to be got rid of are those which disrupt human relationships – those that come between us and those whom we love.

What happens without drugs?

It is extraordinarily difficult to persuade a GP or a psychiatrist to try to initiate the treatment of a schizophrenic unless he is hospitalised. One psychiatrist said to the wife of a severely ill paranoid and angry (though not hallucinated) schizophrenic patient: 'I cannot treat him unless he asks for treatment.' Doctors are afraid of being sued by the patient. I do not believe it to be beyond the realms of possibility for a doctor to do his very best to try, as an outsider, to tell the patient how much happier he and everyone else would be if he took medication and to say that in this way, hospitalisation could be avoided. I do not think doctors try nearly hard enough to help patients in their own homes in order to prevent the very great suffering of patients and their families. The help of a professional outsider who was prepared to help the family by frequent visiting until the patient realised the importance and necessity of treatment would take the burden of responsibility off the family and put the medical responsibility where it should be, with the doctor. The sooner drug treatment is started the quicker will the suffering be ended for all.

However, if the situation cannot be resolved quickly there should be no hesitation on the part of the GP to hospitalise a patient under Section 2 of the Mental Health Act (1983). Even worse, perhaps, than having a patient sent involuntarily to hospital is *not* sending a patient there when his condition warrants it. I received a heart-breaking letter from one woman who was afraid that her highly paranoid husband, who had refused treatment, would kill her. The only suggestion that the doctors could come up with was that she should leave him – they said they had washed their hands of him. But she did not want to become homeless. Another problem for her was a schizophrenic daughter living on her own; whenever the mother went to visit her the husband followed and would bang on the door. The husband drank beer, which even in small quantities is known to exacerbate schizophrenia symptoms. The woman had minimum freedom of movement, yet the doctors would not help either her or her husband by involuntarily placing him in hospital so that the right medical treatment could be given him. It was appalling that this woman and her sick husband had been abandoned by the medical profession, and I wrote to the chief administrator of the health authority concerned to try to bring some pressure to bear. I would encourage patients and their families to study themselves, to try to listen to themselves and to watch their own behaviour, perhaps even tape record themselves and listen to the recording, when they are calm again. Self-knowledge is very important. Even though medication seems an insult to them, patients should, in their rational periods, ask themselves: 'Is it better to go on shouting irrationally at my family because I (in my illness) think they are are at fault or should I try the effect of medication and see if it helps me to return to a normal way of behaviour; in fact to return me to the person I was before the onset of my illness?' This is the single most difficult hurdle to be faced: how to help someone to get well when he does not believe he is ill. There must be solutions

63

we have not yet found. If the patient will not take the necessary medication for the sake of his health or for the protection of others (usually both) then he should be hospitalised involuntarily.

Tragedies are commonplace when a paranoid schizophrenic illness has been left to deteriorate. The patient refuses to believe he is ill, but the family is too afraid to tell him; a downward spiral is then set in motion. By the time the patient has to be taken to hospital the whole affair has become an outrageous public spectacle: ambulancemen and social workers are involved, and the doctors often feel they have to call in the police for their own protection. Fear, chaos and potential for violence are frequent occurrences when a severely ill paranoid schizophrenic has to be taken to hospital. The patient may cut the telephone wires and barricade himself in. Alternatively he may try to run away, resulting in a police chase. The whole situation is quite horrific both for the patient and for his family.

The doctors have created a vicious circle for themselves. As a result of their failure to respond soon enough to the schizophrenic's needs the situation has deteriorated to the point when the police have to be called in. So now the doctors feel they do not want to be involved, and simply tell families: 'If there is any trouble call the police.' The social services can be similarly inept. One very ill patient was staying in lodgings, and his landlady wanted to get rid of him. When she contacted the local social services department they told her to put his pathetic belongings outside on the pavement and to call the police if there was any bother.

Really there is no sensible alternative to medication. There *are* side-effects, unfortunately (see p. 75), and it would be wrong to pretend that some of them are not unpleasant. But today a whole range of drugs is available. If the right one is found for the individual patient, and given in the right dosage for that person, most schizophrenics – like the woman whose story opened this chapter – can live a normal, happy life.

Chemical strait-jackets?

Doctors should realise that every day that passes leaving a paranoid patient unmedicated, causes a deterioration in family relationships which may never be completely healed. Families find it hard to accept that the patient is ill and not bad. If the doctor can find time, and he should make time for such an important subject, he should teach families all he knows about the physical nature of anger, aggression and paranoia. The family's health is usually also his responsibility. He surely does not want to make the family ill by his failure to medicate the patient. That would be, and unhappily often is, total failure on his part. In this country, certain pressure groups, who should know better, talk of neuroleptic medications as 'strait jackets'. They create a climate of opinion wherein paranoid patients echo the cry 'I'm not going to be made into a zombie.' Medication given for medical reasons, because so often badly prescribed, has lost its therapeutic connotation, but it *is* therapeutic, and no one should try to say otherwise, *when well-prescribed*.

The use of neuroleptics has led in an unexpected way to the abandonment of the schizophrenic. After a short stay in hospital he may be drugged up to the eyeballs whilst still full of symptoms, and then discharged to his family or to any other place where society thinks fit to place him. Some of the symptoms may actually derive from poor prescribing of drugs. People should not rush to the facile conclusion that just because a patient has been given drugs he will be able to fend for himself, or even that his family will be able to care for him. Often a lengthy period in hospital is needed; care and education must be given before a patient can be sent home in a mentally stable condition, minimally disturbed by the side-effects of the drugs he has been prescribed. No patient should be discharged if he is still paranoid or suffering from other florid symptoms; unfortunately, with the planned closure of so many psychiatric hospitals in Britain, this is happening more and more.

Family involvement

A few years ago at a conference in Israel I heard a speaker talking about his work as the only psychiatrist in his hospital in the strife-torn Gaza Strip. Nursing staff were few and overstretched, so no psychiatric patient was ever admitted unless a member of his family went with him to look after his immediate needs. Extended families were the norm in the region, and it seemed to me that mental illness was recognized clearly as a disease condition by everyone. The family member who accompanied the patient was accepted as one of the team getting the patient better. When medication was discussed – and it *was* discussed, rather than imposed – the patient and his companion took part. Once the patient was well they both went home, but at the first sign of relapse they went back, or someone from the hospital reassessed the medication, altering it slightly if necessary. The patient was soon back at work, which was expected of him. Why can we not act as humanely – and as practically – in the West?

Treatment before the days of neuroleptics

Clearly there are difficulties surrounding the effective treatment of patients with neuroleptics. So what was it like in the bad old days before the discovery of these drugs – were things relatively so much worse? Insulin and electroconvulsive therapy began to be widely used in the 1930s, when Dr W. A. Cramond was working in a psychiatric hospital in Scotland. In an article published in 1987 he described the state of the patients there before these treatments were available:

> Physical disturbance was common in most wards and a day would rarely pass without some patients requiring physical restraint and an injection of hysocineCo B, to sedate them. Male nurses, in particular, tended to be recruited for size and strength rather than for intelligence and sensitivity. . . . The schizophrenic patient was treated symptomatically – bromides, chloral hydrate, paraldehyde and the range of barbiturates were used for day and night sedation.

He went on to talk about the appearance of the patients as they walked in the morning round the perimeter of the hospital grounds:

> Heads down, shoulders bowed, feet in heavy boots or shoes scuffing the ground as they shamble past. The men are in

ill-fitting tweed suits invariably stained with food; the women in shapeless cotton frocks and woollen cardigans, stockings not infrequently around their ankles. They do not look at you, they seem not to care. Some are muttering to themselves, some have silly, meaningless grins on their faces.

Of all hospital beds available, medical, surgical or maternity, one in four at the time was occupied by a schizophrenic.

Insulin coma was started as a treatment in 1935, and apparently worked best on cases of recent onset. Soon it was all the rage in Europe: studies in Vienna and Switzerland, undertaken on 101 patients, reported complete remission of the disease in 45–50 per cent of cases. After nine months very few patients had suffered a relapse. Insulin coma was given initially because Manfred Sakel of Vienna thought that lowering the blood sugar level might be good for psychoses, and so in order to achieve this he gave his patients insulin.

The first neuroleptics

Nowadays insulin therapy and major brain operations such as leucotomy have been discarded, although electroconvulsive therapy is still used on occasions to treat schizophrenics, and more frequently for depressive patients. In the 1950s the first of the neuroleptics, chlorpromazine, arrived on the scene. Treatments in psychiatry seldom last long, but the neuroleptics seem unlikely to be superseded for some time yet. They undoubtedly offer greater possibilities for success than any of their predecessors, yet, as will be seen on p. 75, they are by no means perfect. Cramond says:

As I look with anxiety at my schizophrenic patients coping with the neurological deficits occasioned by neuroleptic drugs, I not infrequently regret the passing of insulin and wish we could use some other process to provide a re-birthing process into a caring concerned family, safely and yet with some of the attendant drama and anxiety, for I believe that the team anxiety [in giving insulin therapy] played some part in the whole exercise.

The patients treated with insulin in the thirties, he noted, received up to one hundred times as much nursing and medical care as those who were not. Today's peremptory medication and prompt discharge give little time or opportunity for such care and concern.

Chlorpromazine, still in use today and perhaps better known by the proprietary name of Largactil, is a drug with a multitude of uses. It was being investigated for its potential as an anti-histamine when its anti-psychotic properties were discovered; it is also effective against nausea and vomiting, stops persistent hiccuping, lowers blood pressure, and is used in conjunction with anaesthetics to increase their effects. It also has anti-viral properties. It was its ability to sedate patients while still enabling them to remain reasonably alert that first suggested its use in treating schizophrenics. The new drug was remarkably successful, and regarded with great excitement as a major breakthrough.

Later the researchers G. P. Guth and M. A. Spirtes (1964) discovered that phenothiazines, a group of drugs to which chlor-promazine belongs, stabilized membranes of all sorts – this is something that a number of anaesthetics do. In 1986 Dr Guth wrote that 'the accepted orthodoxy now is that the phenothiazines act as antipsychotic agents by antagonising the neurotransmitter dopamine' (see p. 53). He continued by saying that 'When the causes of psychotic derangements were understood, specific therapy would replace the treatment of symptoms offered by the phenothiazines.' Meanwhile it is up to doctors to make the best and most economical use of neuroleptics – and by economical I mean using the least possible dosage consistent with good therapeutic response in order to minimise side-effects.

Dr P. Seeman (1972) took up Guth's point about the effects of phenothiazines on membranes, writing that:

There is a membrane protection at low concentration and membrane lysis (breakdown of tissue) at high concentration. Chlorpromazine is a potent local anaesthetic which suppresses the electrical activity of neurones when applied directly and stabilises membranes in a non-specific fashion, identical to other local anaesthetics. The hypothesis has developed that the apparent specificity of phenothiazines for anti-nausea, anti-psychotic actions results from a particular drug distribution into various brain regions. It is important to point out that if high proportions of chlorpromazine are used all the membranes are disrupted by this surface active drug.

These membrane stabilizing properties of chlorpromazine have been passed over by researchers, and yet they may be important properties in relation to their treatment for schizophrenia. De Lisi et al (1987) wrote a paper on the use of an antiviral agent Acyclovir, to see if it would reduce symptoms of schizophrenia, if schizophrenia were a virally induced illness. They found it ineffective. She did say, however, that there are 'cases of herpes encephalitis and infectious mononucleosis (which) may present with symptoms indistinguishable from schizophrenia.' She also said, and I find this of particular importance, that the neuroleptic haloperidol has anti-viral effects in animals and 'chlorpromazine was reported to have a suppressing effect on the recurrence of herpes simplex infections in humans' (Chang 1975). Thus the list of properties of chlorpromazine continues to grow. It reduces schizophrenic symptoms, is used as a treatment for diarrhoea and has a suppressing effect on viral infections. Are all these effects due, I wonder, to its membrane-stabilizing property?

Neuroleptics today

The drugs prescribed nowadays are divided into a number of different classes, each having different properties and with different side-effects. Authorities in the drug field seem to think there is little to choose between them in their therapeutic use, apart from the fact that some patients respond better to a drug from one class, and some to a drug from another class. There is no way of knowing in advance which drug is likely to suit a particular patient. When a patient has not responded (or has responded badly) to a drug from one class of neuroleptics it is unwise to prescribe another drug from the same class, because the response will probably be no better. Drugs from other classes should be tried first before returning, if necessary, to the original class. The main drugs, divided into their respective classes, are given in the table below, which is taken from the *SAGB Newsletter*. It has been suggested that lithium carbonate should be included in the anti-schizophrenic neuroleptic drug list and as I have noted earlier it is very good for aggressive and violent symptoms as well as for manic depressive illnesses and for mania especially, but also I believe in some cases for depression on its own. It will thus bring down a high mood or bring up a low mood to normal levels. The other neuroleptics are much more complex chemicals as we have seen belonging to a number of different classes. If a patient does not respond to a drug from one class then a drug should be tried from another class, and if he still does not respond, a drug from yet another class should be tested until one is found which is helpful.

Commonly used neuroleptics

Class 1

Phenothiazines

These are divided into three groups depending on the nature of the side-chain in their chemical structure:

	Chemical name	*Proprietary name*
(a) Aliphatic side-chain	chlorpromazine	Largactil, Thorazine
	promazine	Sparine
(b) Piperazine side-chain	trifluoperazine	Stelazine
	perphenazine	Fentazin, Trilafon
	fluphenazine	Moditen, Prolixin
given by injection	fluphenazine decanoate	Modecate
intra-muscularly	fluphenazine enanthate	Moditen
(c) Piperidine side-chain	thioridazine	Melleril
by injection	pipothiazine palminate	Piportil

Class 2

Thioxanthenes

	thiothixene	Norvane
	flupenthixol	Fluanxol
	zuclopenthixol dihydrochloride	Clopixol
given by injection	flupenthixol decanoate	Depixol
intra-muscularly	zuclopenthixol decanoate	Clopixol

70

Class 3

Butyrophenones

| | haloperidol | Serenace, Haldol |
| by injection | haloperidol decanoate | Haldol Decanoate |

Class 4

Diphenylbutylpiperidines

	pimozide	Orap
	fluspiriline	Imap
	penfluridol	Semap

Class 5

Substituted benzamides

| | sulpiride | Dolmatil |

Class 6

Lithium carbonate

| | lithium carbonate | Priadel |

Effects on positive and negative symptoms

Often the negative symptoms of schizophrenia, the apathy, disinterestedness, lack of will to do anything and difficulty in communicating leading to increasing isolation and loss of friends, remain in large measure after neuroleptic treatment. This may indicate that they are relatively untouched by medication, or it may mean that medication is contributing to them. If certain neuroleptics can act like anaesthetics then this property of theirs may induce a state of partial immobility or inertia and apathy anyway. Again, it is a great pity, as I have now repeated several times, that neuroleptic medication is rarely started before the appearance of the florid symptoms. A mild schizophrenic condition should respond to medication more readily than a severe condition.

Dr Stephen Burton, lately medical adviser to Janssen Pharmaceuticals, says that in treating schizophrenics 'Medication balance is crucial.'

By injection

Medications may be given by injection or in tablet form (the oral form of the drug). One or two drugs are in syrup form (haloperidol, for example). It is not considered to be good practice to give a drug by injection and then to give an oral form of the same drug or another oral neuroleptic. The point of giving a drug by injection is to avoid an impasse if a patient either will not take the tablets or if he forgets to take them and is perhaps living on his own, with no one to remind him to take them. Periodic injections, weekly, fortnightly, or monthly overcome this difficulty, but it is my impression and experience that patients quite often feel very much under the weather for about a week after the injection is given. They may feel quite knocked out and able to do nothing but sleep. Towards the end of the time when the next injection is due, and as drug levels fall, there may be a worsening of the illness with an increase in symptoms, leading to disturbance and anxiety within the family, as well as in the patient. Oral medication (tablet or syrup) can result in a more stable condition for the patient with no marked difference in stability over any given period. If however, it is felt that the dosage should be raised or lowered temporarily with the sanction of the doctor, then this is most easily done with tablets. It is more satisfactory if a near relative gives the patient the tablets needed at the right time and also, with the authority of the doctor, looks after the tablets on the patient's behalf, in case he is depressed or suicidal.

Polypharmacy

Polypharmacy, or the prescribing of a number of drugs at the same time, is also much frowned on by those who are experts in pharmacology. The drugs may interact with one another in unknown ways. Nowadays, good medicating means the lowest dose of neuroleptic which gives the maximum therapeutic result. The fewer the drugs, the less complicated will be the process of stabilising the patient and we must remember Professor Parde's (of the National Institute of Mental Health in the USA) comment at the Israel Conference in 1983, that the fewer the metabolites (break-down products) of any one drug, the better. Largactil, for example, has far more metabolites than has Orap. If a number of drugs are given then no one knows what is happening. Polypharmacy is widely deplored yet equally widely practised.

Disipal, Kemadrin or Artane are often given to counteract the side-effects of the neuroleptics. Again, these anti-parkinsonian drugs, as they are known, should not *usually* be taken over a long period of time. Once the body has adjusted to the main medication the anti-parkinsonian drug should be *very gradually* withdrawn *by the doctor*, and not by the patient on his own. Many patients are on these drugs for years and yet they have their own side-effects, and may cause blurred vision and even produce their own contribution to the psychosis *and worsen* the schizophrenia.

However, with the intramuscular drug treatment, the initial dosage of tranquillizers may be so huge and the injection so potent, that sometimes anti-parkinsonian drugs are injected together with neuroleptics. It is perhaps not possible to do without the oral forms of one of these drugs after a neuroleptic injection if it is not injected at the same time as the main medication.

Medication is of such huge importance for schizophrenic patients that it is essential it be prescribed very skilfully. Throughout the years we have found that many members of the SAGB have been very badly medicated. Thus they do not improve as they could and if only doctors tried harder many, many more patients could be made well *now*. Psychiatrists should surely take much more time studying their patients than most of them do to ensure that the maximum therapeutic response to the chosen drug is obtained. Psychiatrists have to maintain close touch with their patients within a hospital setting in order to do this effectively. If they do not get the medication right before discharging the patient they may actually be worse on discharge than before they went in. Medication is nearly always beneficial if correctly and skilfully prescribed. If a patient is discharged whilst still hallucinated, paranoid or otherwise displaying the florid symptoms of disease, his medication has not worked and the psychiatrist must try again *at once*. If there are not enough hospital beds more must be provided and if there are not enough psychiatrists more must be trained.

73

If the patient, on the other hand, is stabilised before discharge everyone, both the patient and his family, will benefit greatly. This should be the practice of psychiatrists universally, but it is not. Very many patients are discharged whilst highly symptomatic.

Kane (1987) has said that giving high dosages of drugs to reduce the length of time in hospital had 'not been shown to shorten the time required for the drugs to exert their therapeutic effect and that four to six weeks was usually necessary or even longer to see the full therapeutic benefits' in treatment-refractory patients. Dr. Kane's recommendation was that 'two or three different classes of anti-psychotic drugs be used for at least four weeks each. Obviously this requires a relatively lengthy period of on-going observation and evaluation. However, there is no shortcut in providing appropriate therapeutic trials in this sub-group. [of treatment-refractory patients].'

Anti-schizophrenic drugs, unlike minor tranquillizers for some people, are not addictive and patients should be reassured by their doctor that this is so, otherwise adverse propaganda may persuade patients that medication should not be taken. It is nearly always beneficial when properly prescribed. I think there is probably an addictive element to anti-parkinsonian drugs and these should be prescribed or withdrawn with particular care.

J. M. Kane, writing in 1987, suggested that the development of neurological side-effects might be used as a guide to identifying the right dosage for a particular patient. He also drew attention to an idea put forward by H. J. Haase and J. Janssen in 1965, which had been neglected by psychiatrists. These two researchers examined the handwriting of patients before and after neuroleptic treatment. When the writing altered due to fine activity of the motor nerves, they found that the optimum therapeutic dose had been reached. Below this level the drug 'does not show any neuroleptic activity but only a tranquillising effect', said Haase, adding that when coarse and noticeable motor activity (as opposed to fine motor activity) occurred there was no further therapeutic advantage and worrying side-effects were also observed. This would be a relatively simple test to organize, and would help ensure that patients' dosages were neither too high nor too low.

It is with much reluctance and considerable dismay that I have had to come to the conclusion that much of the aggression, violence, anger and paranoia of the medicated schizophrenic patient and many of the tragically large and increasing numbers of suicides that take place, may arise as results of poor, badly adjusted neuroleptic treatment. They reflect, I think, a lack of appreciation by many psychiatrists of the delicacy of their task when they use neuroleptics of high potency and dosage to adjust fine chemical balances within the brain. Neuroleptics are often prescribed in too high or too low dosage and in thoroughly undesirable mixtures. This is the polypharmacy deplored by the pharmacists and by such authoritative writers as Kane. Perhaps there should be greater collaboration between pharmacologists and psychiatrists to enable the current neuroleptic treatments to be prescribed with considerably more skill and effectiveness than they are now.

Side-Effects of Neuroleptics

We have seen in the last section that the dosage of a particular drug for a particular patient has to be very exact if the maximum therapeutic level is to be attained. It is with some trepidation thus that I am about to list the many and diverse side-effects produced by neuroleptics if the dosage is not right. Some of these are not serious. Some, on the other hand, may be life-threatening in a tiny percentage of patients. These side-effects were known and reported twenty years ago by Wagensommer (1965), yet there is still much confusion and lack of acknowledgement that they exist, and a disregard for their severity and unpleasantness for many patients. The fact that neuroleptics can themselves produce psychosis, as can anti-parkinsonian drugs, is rarely admitted. There seems no way of discovering which are the symptoms of schizophrenia and which are the side-effects of the drugs given to treat the disease.

There are four types of involuntary (not under the patient's control) motor side-effects. They are known as extra pyramidal effects which depend on the action of the neuroleptics within the nigostriatal system of the brain. They are: parkinsonian effects, akathisia, acute dyskinetic-dystonic reactions and chronic tardive dyskinesia.

75

Parkinsonian effects

These effects come on early in the treatment and resemble the symptoms of Parkinson's disease. Wagensommer (1965) characterized them as 'lack of spontaneous movements and movement accompanying walking, bent stance, restricted shuffling gait and expressionless face. Frequently rigidity and coarse tremor of the hands and feet.' Women, and adolescents of either sex, are more likely to suffer these side-effects than men. Children are less often affected. The symptoms occur, he said, 'in about 4 per cent of patients with weak neuroleptics; 14 per cent with moderately potent neuroleptics; 30 per cent with very potent neuroleptics; and more than 40 per cent with extremely potent neuroleptics'. Even a small reduction of the daily dose is sufficient to reduce the symptoms to a reasonable level, and anti-parkinsonian drugs are helpful in dealing with the problem.

Akathisia

This is a state of enforced motor restlessness which makes the patient incapable of sitting still for more than a short while, and he is happier lying down. Often this side-effect is accompanied by inner agitation. Akathisia is harmless in itself, but still very unpleasant. It occurs in up to 50 per cent of patients taking high-potency neuroleptics, and generally occurs at the start of treatment with high doses.

Acute dyskinetic-dystonic reactions

These are short-lasting symptoms which may nevertheless be very distressing to the patient; they may last from a few minutes to several hours, before subsiding of their own accord. What is called the oculogyric crisis begins with a fixed stare which gives way to a turning upwards of the eyes, followed by hyperextension of the neck. There may be twisting and twitching of the head, and spasms of the jaw and throat muscles: this in turn may lead to the mouth being tightly shut or open, with the tongue protruding. All the symptoms respond to anti-parkinsonian drugs.

Chronic tardive dyskinesia

This name is given to the late-arriving motor side-effects, which consist of virtually continuous movement of the mouth and tongue, and certain postural changes. They occur in about 20 per cent of patients after they have been on neuroleptics for a long while, and may persist for years after all neuroleptic medication has ceased.

Other side-effects

Wagensommer describes many other side-effects, listed here:

Neuroleptics brought on fits in 1.1 per cent of 1534 patients being treated with chlorpromazine.

Weak muscle tone, in contrast to the rigidity of parkinsonism, may result from over-dosage of highly potent neuroleptics.

Frequent disturbances of the autonomic nervous system which regulates the automatic functioning of the main organs of the body such as the heart and lungs are experienced. Dysfunction of the cardio-vascular system is particularly common. An average of 7 per cent of cases treated with promazine or thioridazine showed a marked reduction of blood pressure on circulatory collapse conditions.

There may be exhaustion, weakness in the legs, dizziness, palpitations, or weakness on getting out of bed. Patients may suffer a dry mouth, stuffy nose, blurred vision or flashing lights before their eyes. Thioridazine may cause pigmentation of the retina.

The patient's sex life may be affected since ejaculation can be inhibited. Problems with urination may be experienced, including urgency, incontinence, difficulty in urinating and sometimes complete inability to do so (in which case the drug has to be stopped).

A fall in the white blood cell count may lead to a condition known as agranulocytosis, chiefly in women. It appears to be confined to patients treated with phenothiazines, and a large survey revealed that it only affected about one patient in a thousand. However, since it is a very serious condition, Wagensommer recommended women over forty to have a blood count taken every week.

Jaundice may occur in about 1 per cent of those treated with chlorpromazine. A few cases have developed into cirrhosis of the liver.

Skin problems may occur, such as severe itching, urticaria (nettle rash) and eczema. These may be allergic reactions to the drug.

Phenothiazines often produce oedema (swelling), particularly round the knuckles and on the face – notably the eyelids and mouth.

Women's menstrual cycles may be disturbed: they may have heavy periods, few periods or none at all. Their breasts may swell, and lactation may occur in children as well as in physically mature patients.

Increases in body weight occur sometimes, due to oedema.

Loss of weight may occur because of gastro-intestinal upsets.

Patients on chlorpromazine may be susceptible to heatstroke and sensitive to light.

Confusion and depression are common.

Agitation, irritability, hostility and aggressiveness are not infrequent.

Euphoria may occasionally occur.

Tsuang (1982) says: 'About half the schizophrenics who have been on drug maintenance treatment for two years relapsed' although others disagree and Johnson suggests this figure is less than 20%. Whichever figure is correct both compare 'favourably' says Tsuang 'with an 84% relapse rate in patients who have not been treated.' Ban (1976) commented that 'by now there is sufficient evidence to show that discontinuation of therapy may lead to relapse in between 73% and 95.4% of patients within a year, in between 51% and 75% of patients in six months and in approximately 25% of patients within four weeks.' Groups have been set up called 'Coming off TRANX' (tranquillizers). These have been encouraged by MIND who brought out a booklet about stopping taking minor tranquillizers like valium. Some patients could not be expected to differentiate between minor tranquillizers and major ones, which are the neuroleptics. Consequently patients are reported to have given up their major tranquillizers to the detriment of their health because of the harmful propaganda about mind-bending drugs and strait-jackets. To those contemplating coming off tranquillizers because of so much current propaganda I would say 'DON'T'.

Conclusions

Many members of the Schizophrenia Association of Great Britain, in response to a questionnaire, have sent back lists of their medications. These showed that polypharmacy is widespread. If medication is not given in the least quantity for maximum therapeutic benefit, it is, I am very reluctant to conclude, worse than useless and often very tormenting.

Neuroleptics have been an outstanding treatment for schizophrenia for the past thirty years. They have been remarkable in that for the majority of patients they have alleviated their auditory hallucinations, those destructive voices, and their paranoid delusions, which cause such endless suffering for the patient and his family. What else have they done? They have, according to the American researcher Herbert Meltzer (1987), made some inroads into reducing the less fearsome symptoms of schizophrenia, the so-called negative symptoms of the disease. These are less fearsome because they do not cause the same disruption in relationships as the hallucinations, and especially the paranoia. Nevertheless, it is these negative symptoms which are probably at the heart of the disease.

Thus we need to urge earlier medication, using reduced dosage of neuroleptics. Much more skill is needed in their prescribing. Thirty years is a long time to have been stuck in a groove with a treatment that is far from being wholly beneficial. I think we should call it the dopamine groove. All the time since the discovery of neuroleptics, researchers have pronounced that these neuroleptics act by blocking the dopamine receptors in the brain. Endless research has been carried out on autopsied brain and now with brain scanners, to study dopamine receptors. There is scarcely a backward glance to see what neuroleptics are doing to the rest of the body. There seems to be a mental block in the researchers as well as the dopamine block to which they devote their lives.

However grateful we must be for the development of the neuroleptics, they do not constitute the whole answer for schizophrenia. We have to go a whole lot further. We must not be smug and satisfied about neuroleptics, however great their overall success. We must try to do better. We must have fresh approaches to the treatment of schizophrenia. These will probably devolve from a study of the relationship between gut and brain.

References

BARTKO, G., HERZOG, I. and ZADOR, G., 'Chemical symptomology and drug compliance in schizophrenic patients' in *Acta Psychiat. Scand.*, 77: 74–6 (1988).

CHANG, T. W., 'Suppression of herpetic recurrence by chlorpromazine' in *N. Engl. J. Med.*, 293, 153–4 (1975).

CRAMOND, W. A., 'Lessons from the Insulin story in Psychiatry,' in *Australia and New Zealand Journal of Psychiatry*, 213, 320–6 (1987).

DE LISI, L. E., GOLDIN, L. R., NURNBERGER, J. I., SIMMONS-ALLING, S., HAMOUT, J. and DUIGMAN, C. W., 'Failure to alleviate symptoms of schizophrenia with the novelase of an antiviral agent Acyclovin (Zovinox)' in *Biol. Psychiat.*, 22, 216 (1987).

GREEN, A. R. and COSTAIN, D. W., *Pharmacology and Biochemistry of Psychiatric Disorders*. John Wiley and Sons, Chichester, 1981.

GUTH, P. S., *Current Contents*, 9 February 1987. Citation Classic.

GUTH, P. S. and SPIRTES, M. A., 'The phenothiazine tranquillisers: biochemical and biophysical actions' in *Int. Rev. Neurobiol*, 7, 231–78 (1964).

HAASE, H. J., JANSSEN, A. J. and WAGENSOMMER, *The Action of Neuroleptic Drugs*. Chicago Yearbook Medical Publishers, 1965.

JUDD, L. L., GOLDSTEIN, M. J., RODRICK, E. H. and

JACKSON, N. L. P., 'Phenothiazine effects in good pre-morbid schizophrenics divided into paranoid and non-paranoid status' in *Arch. Gen. Psychiat.* 29, 207–11 (1973).

KANE, J. M., 'Treatment of Schizophrenia' in *Schizophrenia Bulletin*, vol. 13, no. 1 (1987).

MELTZER, H. Y., 'Effect of neuroleptics on the schizophrenic syndrome' in *Clinical Pharmacology in Psychiatry* (eds Dahl, Gran, Paul and Potter). Springer Verlag, Heidelberg, 1987.

PARDES, H., 'Update on Research in Schizophrenia' in *Schizophrenia Bulletin*, vol. 13, no. 1 (1987).

SEEMAN, P., 'The membrane actions of anaesthetics and tranquillizers' in *Pharmacological Reviews*, 24, 4 (1972).

TSUANG, M. T., *Schizophrenia: The Facts*. OUP, Oxford, 1982.

5

SCHIZOPHRENIA AND THE LAW

'It is an odd thing that if you met a man ill-conditioned in body you would not have been angry, but to have met a man rudely disposed in mind provokes you.'

Socrates

Misguided policies

Psychiatric patients may come into contact with the law through the Mental Health Act 1983, which allows patients to be admitted involuntarily to hospital when they are psychiatrically ill and too irrational to understand that hospital treatment can help them to get well. Only 5 per cent of psychiatric patients are hospitalised in this way: the rest are voluntary patients who agree to go into hospital generally at the suggestion of their doctor.

Psychiatric patients may also, of course, encounter the law if they commit criminal acts because of their disturbed brain chemistry. But once these sick people appear in the dock it is the lawyers whose views are taken seriously – even the expert opinion of forensic psychiatrists may be ignored by the courts. Surely there is something wrong with a society that sees fit to punish its mentally ill members by imprisonment, while at the same time it plans for the run-down and eventual closure of many of the big psychiatric hospitals?

It is time to call a halt to present policies. How can psychiatrists be the kind and caring professionals that most of them want to be when their hospitals are being taken from them and their patients pushed out 'into the community' and thence often, via the courts, to prison?

The psychiatric profession must try to get rid of the legal voices interfering – with loudness in direct proportion to their ignorance – in a specialist medical area. If psychiatrists were again to take up full responsibility for their patients they might yet retain the hospitals which are so essential for the safe and compassionate treatment of the mentally sick.

There have only been very few isolated cases of patients being wrongly hospitalised for long periods before the neuroleptic era. Nowadays were more patients to be hospitalised involuntarily their medication could be carefully monitored before their discharge so that they were then well and non-symptomatic. Now as 95% of the patients are in hospital voluntarily they may discharge themselves or be discharged still highly symptomatic. The reasons given for not hospitalising patients involuntarily are (a) financial and (b) doctors are afraid of being sued or being taken to the European Courts. They appear to be content that patients needing hospital should go instead to prison. The fall in the numbers of in-patients in psychiatric hospitals is approximately equalled by the rise in the numbers of the mentally ill in prison.

Psychiatric patients need the same care and devotion – if not more – that is given to other ill people. But now they are being abandoned to an uncaring society by their doctors, some of whom are all too ready, as will be seen later, to let them be sent to prison. British prisons are bulging with psychiatric patients, mostly suffering from schizophrenia, although they may be labelled instead as psychopaths or as suffering from personality disorders. We should be seeking ways of making compulsory hospitalisation easier, quicker and more widely acceptable, rather than regarding it as a shameful process. The civil liberties lobby will probably be up in arms at this statement, but, as I shall explain in due course, where the mentally ill are concerned the situation is more complex than the civil libertarians are prepared to believe. Until earlier diagnosis and effective treatment are the norm many patients will continue to need involuntary hospitalisation for their own well-being and for the common good.

The Mental Health Act 1983: influences and misunderstandings

The major piece of legislation which concerns the mentally ill is the Mental Health Act 1983. Unfortunately there are some widespread misunderstandings about its contents, and it would be as well to explain and dispel these at the outset.

The organization MIND has worked hard on behalf of the mentally ill, and its motives are good – but sadly, as in this instance, its concepts often seem not to work for the good of those whom it seeks to help. In 1975 MIND's legal adviser, an American named Larry Gostin, wrote a book called *A Human Condition – the Mental Health Act 1959–1975;* it constituted MIND's suggestions for amendments to the 1959 Act. The following year the Government published a White Paper entitled *Review of the Mental Health Act 1959*, which was to form the basis of the 1983 Act. Even though some of MIND's ideas were rejected in the White Paper, the fact that those ideas had been aired at all meant that doctors and lawyers, among others, were aware of them, and open to their influence. This situation may well have contributed to the wretched state of psychiatry today.

In some states of the USA 'dangerousness' is a necessary criterion for the involuntary hospitalization of psychiatric patients, but it is not and never has been so in Britain, although many people believe that it is. One suggestion made in the MIND publication was that the admission criteria under the new Act should be 'limited to relate more closely to dangerousness to self or others or to grave disablement'. The White Paper wisely disagreed and said that 'to limit admission to such criteria might be too rigid and could prevent effective treatment being given to people who could benefit but who may be in too confused a state to realise their need'. However, the damage had been done (see p. 87).

Larry Gostin also made the suggestion that relatives should cease to be involved in the admission or discharge of compulsorily detained patients. It was said that, because of emotional involvement, the relative might be unable to see what was best for the patient – the relative might indeed be a contributory factor in the patient's mental disorder. Once again, the White

Paper argued the opposite view, saying that the relatives might have more insight into the patient's likely behaviour and would almost certainly be able to judge better than others whether or not they could cope with the patient. 'It is at present the widely held view', it read, 'that the greater the involvement of the patient's family the better the chances of rehabilitation in the broad sense.' But despite this rebuttal MIND has again sown the seeds of doubt in the minds of those who read both documents. Nowadays relatives are often treated very badly by doctors when all they want is for the patient to be well.

Like most legislation, the Mental Health Act 1983 is lengthy and complex. In this chapter I shall try to explain the main features and implications of its major sections.

Section 4

This Section of the Act allows a patient to be admitted to hospital for assessment in an emergency for seventy-two hours. The application may be made by the nearest relative (see p. 91) or an approved social worker, and needs to be supported by a recommendation from one doctor. Approved doctors must have special psychiatric knowledge and approved social workers are those who have passed special examinations to qualify them for working in psychiatry.

Section 2

This Section allows for twenty-eight days' detention in hospital. An application can be made for admission for assessment, which can include compulsory treatment. The application may be made by the nearest relative or an approved social worker, and needs to be supported by a recommendation from two doctors. The criteria for admission under this Section are:

● That the patient is suffering from mental disorder of a nature or degree which warrants his detention in hospital for assessment (with or without medical treatment)

• That the patient ought to be so detained in the interests of his own health or safety or with a view to the protection of others.

Protection in this sense is interpreted elsewhere in the Act as behaviour which is not physically harmful to the person. Examples of this were given by Larry Gostin and Elaine Rassaby in *Representing the Mentally Ill and Handicapped* as 'family disruption, verbal abuse, public nuisance, damage to property. The distinction is between protection and dangerousness to other people which is limited to physical harm.'

Section 3

This Section allows for initial detention for six months, renewable for a further six months and thereafter annually. The application may be made by the nearest relative or an approved social worker, supported by the recommendation of two doctors, one approved and, if possible, the other with previous acquaintance of the patient. They should not work in the same hospital, unless delay brought about by this requirement would cause serious risk to the health or safety of the patient.

The criteria for admission are:

• That the patient is suffering from mental illness
• That it is necessary in the interests of the patient's health or safety or for the protection of other people that he should be admitted for treatment.

Applying the legislation sensibly

Thus if the nearest relative knows that the mental health of the patient is deteriorating, no other criterion is needed for putting a patient in hospital under the Mental Health Act 1983 than that he requires to be admitted for the sake of his health. If rapid hospitalization on this criterion alone were routine, much suffering and many acts of violence would be prevented.

The danger of the 'dangerousness' concept

Yet MIND's 'dangerousness' idea lingers on very successfully, and has had a pervasive influence on current medical and legal thought. All too often I have heard doctors who have been asked to admit a seriously ill psychiatric patient to hospital counter with: 'Oh, but he isn't dangerous. I haven't seen any evidence of dangerousness. We can't take him into hospital unless he is a danger to himself or others.' In such ways are myths spread throughout the land.

But it is never possible to predict violence. Schizophrenics often do not give the smallest hint of their delusions to the outside world. If they live alone, as did North London mass murderer Denis Nielson, then no one will ever know about their mental condition until they commit criminal acts and are caught. Even if they do not live alone, relatives may be unaware of the severity of the illness, unless perhaps they read the patient's writings. Did Peter Sutcliffe's wife have any idea of his secret killings? Our present understanding of brain chemistry is still evolving – nobody can yet look at another human being and recognize that he or she is harbouring delusions that will lead to the killing or harming of others. Likewise irrational paranoid anger can take hold of the patient and cause him to commit an act of violence, or he may act on the direction of hallucinatory voices, as Sutcliffe did.

Sensibly, then, the criterion of dangerousness is not mentioned in the Mental Health Act 1983 as one required for the involuntary hospitalisation of patients. However, the media are not convinced; dangerousness was discussed in an Esther Rantzen programme (May 1986) as if it were a criterion for hospitalization, and 'Schizophrenics in a Roller-Coaster World', an article that appeared in *Reader's Digest* in June 1987, made the same mistake. I wrote to both Esther Rantzen and the Editor-in-Chief of *Reader's Digest*. The latter replied that he understood 'that MIND felt the working of the Act is open to interpretation and defends the rights of patients not to be committed'.

MIND is wrong; the Act is not open to interpretation in this way. The idea of dangerousness as a criterion was debated during the framing of the Act, and then discarded. When I wrote to the

Department of Health and Social Security about the programme and the article, the reply from Mr R. M. Freeman [Priority Care Division] stated that 'The criteria for detention laid down in the Act, it would appear to me, are clearly worded' . . . and 'dangerousness is not a criterion which must be met before a mentally disordered person can be detained under the Act.' That is surely clear enough for anyone, and the wilful misinterpretation of the Act is the indirect cause of much senseless and avoidable crime by psychiatric patients denied the benefits of hospital treatment. It also denies help to large numbers of patients who are severely ill, but who will never commit crimes and so will never be classed as 'dangerous'.

Who can be detained under the Act?

Those who can be detained, according to the Act, are mentally disordered people, which includes those who suffer from mental illness, mental impairment (mental handicap with special features) and psychopathic disorders. The Act does not define mental illness, but it says that 'psychopathic disorder means a persistent disorder or disability of mind (whether or not including significant impairment of intelligence) which results in abnormally aggressive or seriously irresponsible conduct on the part of person'.

Psychopathy and personality disorders

The terminology used in that part of the Act is worrying. Many SAGB members, as I mentioned in Chapter 1, have been given these labels instead of the proper diagnosis of schizophrenia. This can lead to blurring of distinctions when offences against the law are committed by those with psychiatric problems; and psychopathy has overtones of criminality even if the patient has committed no crime. Once, during a discussion of psychopathy at a medical conference, I asked for a definition of a psychopath and was told by an eminent professor 'It's someone who has no conscience.'

In an attempt to gain more information from official quarters

I wrote in April 1984 to Mr Norman Fowler, then Minister of Health, and to the Medical Research Council. To the Minister I wrote as follows:

As you are aware, the Mental Health Act of 1983 uses the term psychopathic disorder as a diagnosis of mental disorder which may make it appropriate for the patient to receive medical treatment on an involuntary basis in a psychiatric hospital. You must also be aware that many of those now in our prisons are called psychopaths.

As the DHSS must consider psychopathy to be a disease in the real sense of the word, because people are sent for treatment to hospital suffering from it, I would like to know how your Department view psychopathy. What, for example, are its chemical parameters and what research in it is supported by the Medical Research Council? What medications are used in its treatment and what is its prognosis? How is it that so many people given the diagnosis of psychopathy are sent to prison to be punished for acts committed because of mental disorder for which others receiving the same diagnosis are sent to hospital? How is it judged whether there will be a good prospect for treatment benefit?

Personality disorder is another diagnosis frequently made by psychiatrists to patients suffering from mental illness. It is becoming a diagnosis which is increasingly made for patients entering psychiatric hospital, I believe. I believe at the same time the numbers of those given the diagnosis of schizophrenia are diminishing. Could you tell me, please, what is your understanding of the meaning of personality disorder when viewed as a disease condition? Is there any information available about its biochemical parameters? Is it genetically inherited?

Some of our members who have been given the diagnosis of schizophrenia are *later* given a diagnosis of psychopathy or personality disorder by a different psychiatrist. To me this seems totally confusing and harmful to the patient and his family.

The reply included the following remarks:

This Department does not decide what is or is not a disease condition. Section 1 (2) of the Mental Health Act 1983 states that for the purposes of the Act, psychopathic disorder means a persistent disorder or disability of mind (whether or not including significant impairment of intelligence) which results in abnormally aggressive or seriously irresponsible conduct on the part of the person concerned. However, sections 3, 37, 38 and 47 of the Act provide that a patient suffering from psychopathic disorder may only be detained if the disorder is of a nature or degree which makes it appropriate for him to receive medical treatment. The clinical aspects of personality disorder of which psychopathic disorder is a severe form are of course matters for professional judgement and are not matters on which this Department can comment. When Parliament was considering the Mental Health legislation there was much discussion and consultation with interested organisations and the views and practices of professionals in the field played an important part in the framing of the Mental Health Act.

I understand the differential diagnosis between schizophrenia and personality disorder can sometimes give rise to difficulties. It is possible for both conditions to co-exist in the same individual. A psychiatrist may see his patient at a time when he exhibits clinical evidence of schizophrenia, which may be in remission when another psychiatrist sees the patient and recognises evidence of basic personality disorder.

There is a vast amount of literature on the subject of psychopathy to which you may like to refer. The Report of the Committee on Mentally Abnormal Offenders (The Butler Report) addressed itself to the problem of psychopathy and you may find this a useful reference.

I wrote a similar letter to the Medical Research Council (MRC). Their reply said:

The MRC does not at present support any work specifically related to psychopathy and personality disorder. However, as you know the MRC does support a lot of work on schizophrenia, some of which may have relevance for these two conditions.

Unfortunately we do not have any information on the incidence of these conditions but you may find it useful to contact either the Office of Population Censuses and Surveys (Medical Statistics Division) or the Office of Health Economics.

It would not be appropriate for us to comment on whether psychopathy and personality disorder are regarded as disease conditions.

These replies speak for themselves. Why can neither the DHSS nor the MRC comment on whether psychopathy and personality disorder are considered as diseases? Since about half as many patients are in hospital with a diagnosis of personality disorder as there are with a diagnosis of schizophrenia, this seems quite extraordinary. The MRC publication *Research in Schizophrenia 1987* quotes the DHSS *Statistical Bulletin* as showing

a first admission rate for schizophrenia of 6 in 100,000 in 1984 compared to about 15 in 100,000 in the 1950s and 1960s. The reason for this decline has been variously ascribed to changes in diagnosis, an increase in treatment without admission and a fall in real incidence. Similar declines have been recorded in Scotland and Denmark. In Denmark there has been an increase in diagnoses of related conditions at the time of first admission, both in males and females, changing to schizophrenia later on if the condition persists.

I think the fall may in general have come about because patients are increasingly diagnosed as having personality disorders or being psychopathic.

It seems to me incredible that these terms should be used as a way of escape from making a tentative or overt diagnosis of schizophrenia. Having lost many of its sufferers to a rubbish diagnosis that is nevertheless incorporated into the Mental Health Act 1983, schizophrenia is statistically turned into a very much smaller problem; the distortion of the figures does considerable harm to schizophrenia research. And do we want patients to enter the prison system because of these misapplied labels? That is undoubtedly what is happening, with ever greater frequency.

The nearest relative

To return to the specifics of the Mental Health Act 1983, here, in descending order, is the list of nearest relatives who can apply for involuntary hospitalization:

- Husband or wife
- Son or daughter
- Father or mother
- Brother or sister
- Grandparent
- Grandchild
- Uncle or aunt
- Nephew or niece
- Where the person would be the nearest relative other than the husband, wife, father or mother of a patient and is for the time being under 18 years of age, the nearest relative of the patient shall be ascertained as if that person were dead.

L. Kuiper and P. Bebbington (1987) define the nearest relative as

the one with whom the patient lived before going into hospital. Where there is more than one such person or the patient lives alone, the legal nearest relative is the one closest to the top of the list. A cohabitee may qualify as the nearest relative if he or she has lived with the patient for at least six months as husband or wife unless there has been a legal separation or divorce. A person other than a relative who has lived with the patient for at least five years counts as a relative but in the last position on the list.

Before a compulsory admission is made, the patient must have refused voluntary admission to hospital.

The patient's rights: Leaflet 7

If a patient is discharged after admission under a section of the Mental Health Act 1983 his nearest relative must be informed, unless either that relative or the patient has requested otherwise. The hospital managers have to tell involuntary patients of their right to appeal to a Mental Health Review Tribunal (MHRT) if they do not want to be detained in hospital. This must be done within fourteen days of an admission under Section 2 (twenty-eight-day order); and within the first six months, second six months and thereafter annually if the patient is held under Section 3. Relatives can also discharge patients by giving seventy-two hours' notice in writing to the hospital managers. If the hospital does not agree, the relative can then refer the patient to a MHRT.

It seems to me entirely unreasonable to put the patient and his family through the trauma of an involuntary hospitalization under Section 2 and then, before he has had time to get better, to ask him if he would like to appeal for his discharge. If, as is usually the case, the patient has been angry and hostile towards his family before being admitted to hospital, they have every reason to fear his rapid return if the MHRT discharges him. No one seems to thinks of the needs (I have deliberately avoided using the word 'rights') of the relatives to recover from the often harrowing and exhausting experience of living for a prolonged period with someone who is acutely psychotic. Legal intervention through MHRT in the early stages of the medical treatment of a severely ill schizophrenic can, I think, do nothing but harm; it can cause great uncertainty and disruption to the patient, to his family, and to medical and nursing staff.

Psychosurgery and the surgical implantation of hormones may never be performed without the patient's consent and a second medical opinion. This is also the case for voluntary patients.

All this information is included in Leaflet 7, a copy of which is given to patients held under Section 3 and to their nearest relative. This document is printed below in its entirety:
NB. Leaflet 7. This is a copy specifically given for section 3 patients. Section 2 patients undoubtedly have a different leaflet.

Mental Health Act 1983 Leaflet 7
Section 3

Name ....

Your hospital doctor is ....

Date of admission ....

Your Rights under
the Mental Health Act 1983

Why you are being held
You are being held in this hospital/mental nursing home on the advice of two doctors. You can be kept here for up to 6 months so that you can be given the treatment and care that

you need. You can only be kept in hospital for longer than 6 months if your doctor thinks you need to stay. If your doctor thinks you should stay longer he will talk to you about this towards the end of the 6 months.

You must not leave unless a doctor tells you that you can. If you try to leave before then the staff can stop you, and if you do leave you can be brought back. You can be held in this way because of Section 3 of the Mental Health Act 1983. These notes are to tell you what that means.

If you want to leave
The doctor will tell you when he thinks you are well enough to leave hospital. If you want to go before the end of the 6 months, or before he says you are ready, you will have to get the agreement of either

the hospital managers; or

the Mental Health Review Tribunal

If you think you should be allowed to leave hospital you should talk to your doctor. If he thinks you should stay, but you still want to leave, you can ask the hospital managers to let you go. You should write to them to ask them to do this. Their address is ....

The Tribunal
You can also ask the Mental Health Review Tribunal to decide if you can leave hospital. You can ask the Tribunal to look at your case by writing to them or sending them a form which the hospital can give you. The Tribunal's address is ....

You can apply to the Tribunal any time in the next 6 months and if you withdraw your application you can apply again. If you need help writing the letter or filling in the form your social worker or the hospital staff will help you.

There are usually three people on the Tribunal – a lawyer, a psychiatrist (doctor) and a third person who is not a doctor. All these people will come from outside the hospital.

If you ask the Tribunal to look at your case they will probably ask to see you and your doctor. If the Tribunal see you, they will be able to make sure that they have full details of your case, and you will be able to tell them yourself why you want to leave hospital. You may not have to see the Tribunal if you do not want to but you can insist on seeing them if you want. The doctor from the Tribunal will want to talk to you in any case. The Tribunal will listen to what you and your doctor say, and to what everyone else says, and then decide if you can leave hospital.

You can also ask someone, including a solicitor if you wish, to help you to ask the Tribunal to look at your case and help you put your views to the Tribunal. Because of the legal advice and assistance scheme this Tribunal office or social worker will tell you how to find a solicitor or other help if you ask them.

If you have not applied after 6 months, the hospital managers will apply for you. If your doctor advises that you need to stay in hospital for a further 6 months you will be able to apply again. After that you can apply every year you are still kept in hospital under the Mental Health Act.

Your treatment
You are being kept in hospital to make sure that you get the medical treatment you need. Your doctor will talk to you about any treatment he thinks you need. In most cases you will have to accept his advice except in the case of certain treatments.

If your doctor wants you to have certain very specialised and rare treatments he *must* have your agreement and he must get another doctor's opinion on the treatment that he wants you to have. You can withdraw your agreement at any time. The other doctor will have to talk to other staff who are involved in your case, including a nurse. The law protects you in other ways too. If your doctor wants you to have one of these treatments he will explain all this to you.

If your doctor feels that you need to have ECT (electro convulsive therapy, sometimes called electric shock treatment) and you agree, he can go ahead with the treatment. But if you do not agree, unless it is an emergency, he must first ask a doctor from outside the hospital to see you. This other doctor will talk to you and to other staff who are involved in your case, including a nurse, about the treatment and decide whether you need it. If the second doctor says you should have this treatment you will be given it.

95

If at first you agree that your doctor may give you ECT but later you change your mind you should tell your doctor that you no longer agree to this treatment. He will then have to ask a doctor from outside the hospital to see you, to decide whether you need to go on having it. Again, he will talk to other staff.

Your doctor will talk to you about any medicine or drug treatment he thinks you need. You must accept the treatment for the first 3 months that you are kept in hospital under the Mental Health Act. (If you are not given any medicines or drugs at first, the 3 months only begins when your doctor starts to give you them.) If after 3 months your doctor wants you to carry on having any drug treatment or medicine he must, except in an emergency, get your agreement first. If you agree he can continue the treatment. But if you do not agree, he must ask a doctor from outside the hospital to see you. This other doctor will talk to you and to other staff who are involved in your case, including a nurse, about the treatment and decide whether you need it. If the second doctor says you should have this treatment, you will continue to be given it.

If when the 3 months is up you at first agree that your doctor can carry on giving you any medicine or drug treatment but later you change your mind, you should tell your doctor. He will then have to ask a doctor from outside the hospital to see you and decide whether you need to go on having it. Again, he will talk to other staff.

If you have any questions or complaints

If you want to ask something, or to complain about something, talk to the doctor, nurse or social worker. If you are not happy with the answer you may write to the hospital managers. If you are still not happy with the reply you are given you can ask the Mental Health Act Commission to help you. You can also write to the Commission even after you have left hospital.

The Mental Health Act Commission

The Commission was set up specially to make sure that the mental health law is used properly and that patients are cared for properly while they are kept in hospital. You can ask them to help you by writing to them at ....

Your letters
Any letters sent to you will be given to you. You can send letters to anyone except a person who has said that he does not want to get letters from you. Letters to these people will be stopped by the hospital.

Your nearest relative
A copy of these notes will be sent to your nearest relative who we have been told is ....

If you do not want this to happen please tell the nurse in charge of your ward or a doctor. Your nearest relative can write to the hospital managers to ask them to let you leave. The managers will need at least 72 hours (3 full days) to consider such a request, so that they can get a report from your doctor. Only one request will be considered in any one period of 6 months. If your doctor reports that you should not leave, your nearest relative can ask for a Tribunal to look at your case.

If there is anything in this leaflet you do not understand, the doctor or a nurse or social worker will help you. If you need help in writing a letter you should ask one of them, or a relative or friend.

Guardianship

The concept of guardianship was introduced to enable help such as medical treatment, social support and training to be given to someone who would not seek it on his own account.

Section 7: Application for Guardianship

An application for guardianship can, in the words of Section 7, be made on these grounds:

• That the patient is suffering from mental disorder, being mental illness, severe mental impairment, psychopathic disorder or mental impairment.
• That it is in the interests of the welfare of the patient that he should be received [into guardianship].

Two medical recommendations are required. The application may be made by the nearest relative or an approved social worker (who must consult the nearest relative if it is possible to do so).

Section 8: Effect of Guardianship Application

A guardianship application confers upon the local social services department or the person named as guardian the following powers, as stated in Section 8:

• To require the patient to reside in a place specified by the authority or person named as guardian.
• To require the patient to attend at places and times specified for the purpose of medical treatment, occupation, education or training.
• To require access to the patient to be given at any place where the patient is residing, to any registered practitioner, approved social worker or any other person to be specified.

Patients Concerned in Criminal Proceedings or Under Sentence

Under Sections 35, 36, 37 and 38 the Act provides for offenders to be transferred to hospital if they are mentally disturbed.

Section 35: Remand to hospital for report on accused's mental condition

The Crown Court or a Magistrate's Court may remand an accused person to a hospital specified by the Court for a report on his mental condition. The powers may be exercised if the Court is satisfied, on the written or oral evidence of a registered medical practitioner, that there is reason to suspect that the accused person is suffering from mental illness, psychopathic disorder, severe mental impairment or mental impairment. . . . The Court shall not remand an accused person to a hospital unless satisfied that arrangements have been made for his admission to *that hospital* and for his admission to it within the period of seven days beginning with the date of remand. An accused person shall not be remanded for more than 28 days at a time or for more than 12 weeks in all.

Section 36: Remand of accused person to hospital for treatment

The Crown Court may, instead of remanding an accused person in custody, remand him to a hospital specified by the court if satisfied, on the written or oral evidence of two registered medical practitioners, that he is suffering from mental illness or severe mental impairment of a nature or degree which makes it appropriate for him to be detained in hospital for medical treatment. An accused person shall not be remanded or further remanded under this section for more than 28 days at a time or for more than 12 weeks in all.

Section 37: Hospital and Guardianship Orders: Powers of courts to order hospital admission or guardianship

Where a person is convicted before the Crown Court of an offence punishable with imprisonment . . . or is convicted by a magistrate's court of an offence punishable on summary conviction with imprisonment . . . the court may by order authorise his admission to and detention in such hospital as may be specified in the order, or as the case may be, place him under the guardianship of a local social services authority or of such other person approved by a local social services authority as may be so specified.

Section 38: Interim hospital order

Where a person is convicted before the Crown Court of an offence punishable with imprisonment . . . the Court may, before making a hospital order or dealing with him in some way, make an order (in this Act referred to as 'an interim hospital order') authorising his admission to such hospital as may be specified in the order.

Section 135: Warrant to search for and remove patients

If it appears to a justice of the peace, on information on oath by an approved social worker, that there is reasonable cause to suspect that a person believed to be suffering from mental disorder:

a) has been, or is being, ill-treated, neglected or kept otherwise than under proper control in any place within the jurisdiction of justice, or

b) being unable to care for himself, is living alone in any such place,

the justice may issue a warrant authorising any constable named in the warrant to enter, if need be by force, any premises . . . to remove him to a place of safety . . . for his treatment and care.

Aftercare for involuntary patients

When a patient is discharged after compulsory hospitalisation the local health authority and social services department must by law provide aftercare. Patients and mentally disordered offenders must be found somewhere to live, and must be cared for by health and social services workers.

Voluntary patients

Voluntary patients who agree to go into hospital can refuse treatment once there and discharge themselves. Often a merry-go-round situation arises when the patient keeps going into hospital and discharging himself before his condition has stabilised. It may even deteriorate if he has refused medication whilst there. There is no obligation on Social Services or the District Health Authority to look after such patients if officially discharged or if they discharge themselves. This applies to 95% of patients, we must remember. It is often almost as difficult to persuade a patient to go into hospital voluntarily as it is to get him through a Section of the Mental Health Act. Additionally, if a doctor fails to get the agreement of the patient, he may be very angry with his family when the doctor has gone, for calling him in the first place. I will have more to say about voluntary patients shortly, but first would like to comment further on Mental Health Tribunals and the Mental Health Commissioners who are again only concerned with the 5% of involuntary patients. The other 95% are no-one's responsibility once they have left hospital.

The Mental Health Commission

Set up in 1983, the Commission has 97 commissioners, mostly lawyers, doctors, nurses, psychologists and social workers. Leaflet 7 explains that the Commission was set up to make sure that the Act is adhered to correctly, and that patients in hospital are cared for properly. The commissioners investigate the complaints of involuntary patients through hospital visits, and even after such patients have left hospital. They arrange for doctors' second opinions to be given where controversial treatments like psychosurgery or hormone implants are suggested.

In 1988 the eminent lawyer Mr Louis Blom-Cooper was appointed its second chairman, and a *Guardian* article (September 28 1988) by Melanie Phillips commented on the problems facing the new incumbent. For a start, the Commission had overspent its £700,000 budget by 10 per cent. Commissioners, unless they were NHS employees, were currently paid about £90 a day plus expenses when on Commission work: one member was estimated to be earning £26,000 a year.

The article went on to say that Mr Blom-Cooper was disquieted 'over the code of practice, the statutory guidance to the working of the Mental Health Act which the Commission had to write. It produced a draft *without* consultation with the Royal College of Psychiatrists some of whose members had been hostile to the Act in the first place and which promptly rubbished the code. The DHSS then wrote a second draft. This was found unacceptable and it was now writing a third draft [and] desperately trying to persuade the warring factions of psychiatry and civil liberties that the code was not making new law but was simply a guide to the existing statute. Blom-Cooper was distraught at the poisonous relationship between the Commission and the psychiatrists.'

Sometimes, apparently, as many as thirty commissioners had descended on a psychiatric hospital. This must have considerably upset the everyday work of the hospital and prevented the doctors from getting on with the job of treating the patients. No wonder psychiatrists are angry.

Lawyers should meddle as little as possible in psychiatry. Altogether I think the Mental Health Commission is a bad idea. The doctors are the specialists in psychiatry. There are some doubts already about its future. It may well be in the balance.

What's wrong with the law?

In July 1983 a joint meeting was held by MIND and the Legal Action Group (LAG) on the practice and procedure of MHRTs; this was in anticipation of the expected rush of patients who would apply for their discharge when the 1983 Act came into force on 30 September that year. A patient formally detained under Section 25 of the 1959 Mental Health Act (which is equivalent to Section 2 in the 1983 Act) was not allowed to appeal to a MHRT. Now also patients can apply for legal aid to get a solicitor to represent them at a Tribunal if they cannot afford to pay. MIND was, and still is, encouraging patients to apply for legal representation at MHRTs. Remember, within the first fourteen days of hospitalisation under Section 2 of the Act any litigious, paranoid patient (who will probably still be very ill) is told he can apply to a MHRT for his discharge. With a clever lawyer to represent him he may well get it, but at the expense of not regaining his mental health.

That conference room was brimming with bright young lawyers (but very few doctors), who had come to learn how to represent the mentally ill at tribunals. They seemed to think that the freedom of the individual was all that mattered. But this was

not a simple black and white, right or wrong situation. Many
lives can be ruined by lawyers who take no account of the fact
that a patient suffering severe mental illness does not have the
capacity for a full, rewarding and happy life. During a break in
the proceedings, I reminded one of the lawyers that the policy
of discharging patients precipitously often led to their eventual
loss of freedom through prison. He turned to me with a cynical
look and said, 'Does it matter?' Civil liberties ring rather hollow
without the mental health to go with them.

At one stage an imaginary case was used for a role-playing
game: members of the audience were given parts to play in a
mock tribunal. The Social Worker said he had no accommodation
to provide for the patient. The audience laughed. The Relative
said, 'No, the patient cannot come home.' The audience laughed
again. It would appear that the lawyers' brief is to get the patient
out of hospital at whatever cost in terms of suffering to the patient
and his family.

Nor is the cost just in terms of suffering. If legal aid is not
granted, big lawyers' bills may create financial hardship. One
MHRT cost the patient over £500, which included £65 for independent medical advice. The fees would have been higher still if
a social worker's report had been requested (which MIND thinks
is advisable). One legal representative recommended by MIND
said that the increased numbers of tribunals would bring in fat
fees for the lawyers. He also remarked to a public meeting which
I attended that he had 'sprung' a patient from a high-security
unit in a psychiatric hospital – to the dismay of her consultant.
That patient was back in hospital again within days. Surely the
lawyer's action was quite contrary to the spirit of the Act.

One patient of my acquaintance, represented by a firm of
solicitors recommended to him by MIND, was discharged by a
MHRT. The tribunal members consisted of a lawyer as chairman,
a psychiatrist and a layman. The legal representative was present
throughout, and yet no witnesses were allowed to be. They gave
evidence singly. This was because the hearing was an informal
one. Had it been formal, as originally intended, they could all
have been present thoughout the hearing. At the last minute
the legal representative had persuaded the patient to change his
mind and have this informal hearing – mainly, he said, because

it would be quicker and therefore cost less. (This, incidentally, was the tribunal with the £500-plus fee – even the cheaper form of tribunal represented a lot of money to the patient and his family).

The patient could be discharged if the tribunal members were unanimous, or if there were a majority of two to one. Unfortunately the composition of the tribunal was, in my view, unbalanced. The psychiatrist might have supported the Responsible Medical Officer (RMO) who gave evidence supporting his wish not to discharge the patient, but could have been over-ruled by the non-medical members who might easily have been persuaded by the legal representative to discharge against medical advice. Like the lawyers at the conference described above, the representing solicitor saw his brief as being to get the patient out of hospital whatever his mental condition, just as if he were representing someone up before the magistrate for a traffic offence.

Whatever the eventual voting in this case, the patient was discharged. Yet a few days later he was picked up by the police, who found him in a confused state of mind in someone's garden shed. He was unmedicated and uncared for. The following week he was described by two GPs as 'completely mad', and said to be living in an indescribable mess. Fortunately for him he did not end up in prison but in another psychiatric hospital – after several weeks of sheer hell for him and his family.

The right to hospitalization

In *The Health Services* of 24 December 1982, John Wilder of the Psychiatric Rehabilitation Association wrote an article about the discharged mentally sick wandering our streets:

> We might all reject the processes of institutionalisation but we must also recognise that many patients rendered inadequate by their illness are being realistic to respond to hospital life with its order and security as compared to the cut and thrust of a greedy society outside. Unfortunately for them, the concept of 'asylum' is fast disappearing. Psychiatrists are now saying in effect that if, in their clinical judgement, they have done

all they can for a patient, then it becomes the responsibility of the community to take care of them.

He cited the case of a psychotic patient discharged home from a psychiatric hospital twenty-five miles away. The patient became suicidal, but was refused admission to the local psychiatric unit because he was 'not their responsibility'. Shortly afterwards he jumped out of his bedroom window. Another patient was refused admission because when he was ill he was, as the duty doctor put it, a nuisance. This normally kind, quiet patient drowned himself in despair.

'It makes nonsense', said John Wilder, 'of the Hippocratic Oath to discharge long-term vulnerable psychiatric patients knowing that this cavalier treatment leads to relapse or at best survival without complaint because the illness and cocktail of drugs [polypharmacy] prescribed also reduce the critical faculties.' He then quoted Dr Roger Morgan:

Schizophrenia contributes more and institutionalisation contributes less to the residual state of chronic schizophrenic disability than is generally believed. If accepted . . . it would be legitimate to keep schizophrenics in hospital for as long as was indicated for thorough treatment of their primary illness in an environment carefully designed for that purpose. Premature discharge would be recognised as ill-judged and unnecessary. Patients and their relatives would be spared much avoidable suffering.

In an article about violence in an American quarterly called *Getting Better*, the case of John Hinkley – the man who tried to assassinate former President Reagan – was used as an example. He had been receiving therapy for anxiety, but the treatment seemed to make him worse (was he being given the wrong drugs?). His parents appealed to his psychiatrist to admit him to hospital, but to no avail. The writer then used the most hopeful phrase I have heard for a long time: 'Why', he asked, 'was this young man not accorded the right to hospitalisation. . . .?'

A hospital must always be a refuge, an asylum and a place of treatment. Those who seek to abolish our large psychiatric hospitals for the sake of the freedom of the individual are doing more harm than good. 'Let the mentally ill live in the community' is the cry – but many of these seriously ill patients, deprived of their right to hospitalization, will end up in prison. And the protagonists of freedom for the mentally ill will not be there to help them then.

E. Tanay (1987) published a paper called 'Homicidal Behaviour in Schizophrenics', in which he wrote about the American experience – not so very different from that in Britain:

> This paper emphasises that homicidal behaviour may be part of the clinical manifestation of schizophrenia. The failure to hospitalise potentially violent schizophrenics contributes to the incidence of psychotic homicide. The tendency to diagnose homicidal behaviour as personality disorders combined with legal changes [in the USA] brought about a shift of this population from the mental health system to the criminal justice system. Accounts of killings by psychotics often begin with a reassurance that psychotics rarely kill. . . . In the past psychotics even though homicidal rarely caused death since they were confined to psychiatric institutions . . . unpredictable violence is a common symptom of psychosis. . . . The homicidal tendencies of schizophrenics and other psychotics are often neglected or denied. Schizophrenics who engage in violence are at times diagnosed as personality disorders.

So the same escape clause is used in the USA as in Britain.

Even when patients *are* hospitalized in Britain, under the Mental Health Act 1983 the unpleasant and destructive rigmarole initiated by early discharge can be repeated endlessly – the only people who seem to gain are the lawyers. Psychiatrists are being intimidated by the law at every turn, and it is easy to envisage a future in which no psychiatrist will be prepared to send a patient to hospital under any Section of the Act, and in which very many seriously ill patients will commit all sorts of crimes because of their disturbed brain chemistry. Is it right that patients, their families, and society in general should be put at risk in this way, while irresponsible lawyers line their own pockets?

Prison: the unacceptable alternative

Because of the horrific nature of their crimes, some people – like Peter Sutcliffe – are not allowed by the lawyers to be regarded as mentally ill. Dr Hugo Milne, a forensic psychiatrist specializing in the mentally ill criminal offender, examined Sutcliffe and found him to be a severe case of paranoid schizophrenia. He said: 'We may not know what causes schizophrenia any more than we know what causes cancer. But that man is schizophrenic and he is in the wrong place. We are back to the old situation where medicine communicates with law and law communicates with medicine, and the law only accepts what it wishes.' But Sutcliffe was tried and sent to prison, despite the expert forensic evidence. He has since been transferred to Broadmoor, one of Britain's four top-security hospitals.

Even some doctors may lose sight of the fact that their patients are ill, and may be persuaded that disturbed behaviour should be punished by law rather than treated by medicine. For example, not long ago a very ill patient broke the glass top of a door in a secure unit in a hosital. In due course he was sent to prison because of his action. The fact that a patient can be transferred from hospital to prison because of his disturbed behaviour in hospital is a bitter irony, and shows the poverty of thinking in current attitudes to the mentally ill.

Very recently it was reported that psychiatric patients in prison would now receive better medical treatment: 'New Prison Deal for Mentally Ill' was the headline to a *Guardian* (September 16 1988) article by Stephen Cook. He reported that

> An initiative is underway in the prison service to help mentally ill and mentally handicapped offenders by segregating them and giving them better medical treatment. Over the next three years between twelve and twenty low-security prisons will have special wings set aside for mental cases, staffed mainly by prison officers who are either registered general or mental nurses.

The patients who would occupy such prison wings would be 'chronic schizophrenics, people with mild mental handicap and some psychopaths who are not considered dangerous'.

But there should never be a prison deal for the mentally ill, because they should never be in prison in the first place. The growing acceptance that it does not matter whether the sick person ends up in hospital or prison is quite outrageous. Expediency and economy seem to be the criteria used, not the needs of the patient.

One further comment on the current treatment of the mentally ill in prison is that they are given medication only if they agree to do so voluntarily. If they refuse to take it, in other words, they may be left in a mentally deteriorating condition. The argument has been put to me that it would be interfering with their human rights to be forced to take medication. But surely imprisonment of the mentally ill is a deprivation of all rights – even of the right to treatment in order to be made well. Until we reject this policy, we shall not become a civilized society.

References

Review of the Mental Health Act 1959, HMSO, London, 1976.
The Mental Health Act, HMSO, London, 1983.
GOSTIN, L. O., *A Human Condition: The Mental Health Act 1959–1975 (MIND)*. NAMH, London, 1977.
GOSTIN, L. O. and RASSABY, E., *Representing the Mentally Ill and Handicapped*. Quatermaine House, 1980.
KUIPER, L. and BEBBINGTON, P., *Living with Mental Illness*. Souvenir Press, London, 1987.
TANAY, E., 'Homicidal behaviour in schizophrenia' in *Journal of Forensic Science*, vol. 32, no. 5, 1382–8 (1987).

6

LIVING WITH A SCHIZOPHRENIC

The possibility of a life-enhancing experience

Living with someone whose schizophrenia is controlled with minimal medication of the right sort can be interesting, exciting and unpredictable. Schizophrenics are often artistic: they may paint, sculpt, write prose or poetry, or play music. They may invent things, or be geniuses with engines and computers. They may like to talk through the night on impossible philosophical topics. They may have unexpected insight and understand others perhaps better than they understand themselves. There is nothing dull about living with a *well* schizophrenic – life can be a real adventure.

The problems of premature discharge from hospital

Unfortunately, nowadays that possibility is becoming ever more distant. The Government's policy of running down psychiatric hospitals is leading to the discharge, into the care of their families, of many schizophrenic patients who are still full of symptoms. Those families were often accused by psychiatrists of having caused the disease in the first place, and hurried efforts are currently being made to deny this hypothesis. Presumably this is for expediency's sake: once the hospitals close, the (untrained) families will be needed to act as full-time psychiatric nurses to patients who were not well enough to have been discharged in the first place.

The fact that the discharge of so many symptom-ridden patients

109

seems acceptable to the authorities means that it may no longer be possible for families to find a valid reason for hospitalizing them again. Schizophrenics, it appears, must just learn to live with their chronic symptoms. Likewise relatives must learn to expect little help or encouragement in improving the health of the patient (or in lessening their own burden when the illness is severe) by getting him easily into hospital. I. H. Minas and his colleagues (1988) wrote of thirty-two discharged patients whom they investigated; over half still had hallucinations and a quarter had thought disorder. They point out an obvious flaw in the logic of the present system:

> It may be argued that in severely ill schizophrenic patients it is not necessary that acute psychotic symptoms be completely resolved before discharge, and that treatment can be continued by the community or home-based services . . . [But] given that such a large proportion of the patients in this sample had continuing positive psychotic symptoms, what is the probability that, following discharge, they would attend follow-up appointments and comply with maintenance medication? It is commonly observed that when such patients *are* re-admitted, a substantial proportion has not complied with follow-up arrangements made at the time of the last discharge or with maintenance anti-psychotic treatment.

These authors quote S. Reibel and M. Herz (1976), who said that 'persistent poor judgment and impulsive behaviour . . . anti-social behaviour patterns and continued psychotic disorganisation, clearly limit the effective post-discharge adaptation as well as the family's and community's capacity to accept and tolerate discharged patients'. Yet, as we have seen, the false cry is: 'He is not a danger to himself yet. Wait until evidence occurs and then he can be hospitalized – or imprisoned.' Looking after a very ill schizophrenic out of hospital results in agony for everyone, including the patient.

Here are two case histories. In the first, a wife tells of her husband's behaviour on discharge:

> He was highly deluded and suffering quite marked neurological symptoms. He shouted nonsense in a tremendous voice, saying

things like: 'Do you take orders from the bloody cats?' He
created great chaos and havoc. He sprayed the wall outside the
house with a paint aerosol; he sprayed on to a large painting
the words: 'Feed my lambs'. He let down a neighbour's car
tyres. He barricaded the entrance to the garden. He was
literally raving in an absolutely gigantic voice – superhumanly
loud it seemed.

This is a woman's description of the events leading up to her
brother's suicide, written the day after his funeral:

Three months later he was discharged to live at home with
my parents, who both work full-time. He gradually reduced
his tablets until he was off them altogether . . . Initially he had
regular visits from a psychiatric nurse; but these had come to
an end despite my mother's protests. The visits of an informed
professional had been and would have continued to be a great
help; this nurse was a fine and caring man.

Early this summer my brother had a good phase. This ended
when my parents were on holiday. He came to visit us whilst
they were away; this was to be the last time I saw him.

When my parents returned he was unwell and not talking
to them. My mother attempted to get medical help when he
indicated that he wanted it, but to no avail. It seemed that
because he had not attended his out-patients' appointments
no one was interested.

Do these people in all sincerity, knowing what they do
about schizophrenia really expect such patients to attend these
appointments? I cannot believe that they do. It seems to me to
be a convenient way of letting people drop out of the system
and later blaming them for it.

This is the way it continued for the last couple of months
until last week. At 1 a.m. last Thursday morning he knocked
on my parents' bedroom door and told them he felt ill. They got
up and made some tea and talked. Later my mother rang the
GP on night duty, who rang back at 3 a.m. She was cross at
being woken at that time of night and said there was nothing
she could do to help, even though my mother had explained
the situation to her.

111

My parents were – indeed still are – very upset at what we all consider to be a professional misjudgment. All the doctor had to do was talk to my brother, say that she would get help that day, and possibly give him a sleeping tablet. My brother was desperate, we now know.

They all returned to bed. Later my brother got up and went out of the house. My parents went after him but failed to find him. When they returned home they found him lying in bed listening to music, unaware that he had ever left the house. My mother said that she would sort out a doctor in the morning.

Later my parents left for work. My mother spent the morning on the telephone trying to get an appointment with the consultant psychiatrist, even offering to pay. She rang her GP (not the one who had been on night duty), who was furious about the situation. She later phoned my mother – having obtained an appointment for my brother at 3 p.m.

Just as my mother was arranging to leave for home she received a phone call from my brother. He said, 'Mum, I've done it.'

'No, I've got an appointment,' she said. 'I'm coming.'

My mother returned home immediately with a friend. My brother's room, the stairs and the hall where the phone is were covered in blood. My mother's doctor was adamant that if my brother was found he would live. She was with my parents when they received the news that he had been found on the railway line. His mental and physical suffering had come to an end.

In the first case it was obvious that the patient was much too ill to have been discharged; he and his family were overwhelmed by the severe symptoms he still exhibited. In the second case the patient would not have committed suicide had he been rapidly transferred to hospital and given drugs. What is the good of a policy of community (in other words, family-based) care if the results are a nightmare?

Confusion of cause and effect

Here is a shocked psychiatrist's response to a recently hospitalized patient who had been living 'in the community', which for him at this particular time meant on his own.

He became increasingly aggressive verbally and even thumped the table on several occasions, literally thrusting his face and clenched fists in front of me. He issued orders to patients and staff and refused to take any advice or medication. He continued to be demanding, dictatorial, unpleasant, argumentative and explosive, and refused to co-operate. He had no insight into his illness and felt he was being treated unfairly and imprisoned in hospital.

Not very long before, the patient had been discharged from another hospital and his wife had been advised to obtain an injunction to prevent him from coming home. Another psychiatrist commented: 'His mental illness is largely exacerbated by the explosive and stormy marital conflict and their tremendous clash of personalities.'

The first psychiatrist had been devastated by the patient's behaviour within a secure hospital setting. I wonder how the wife could have been expected to remain calm within the family home, where no help would have been available had she been attacked. He continued:

In view of his long-standing intractable mental illness, his marital disharmony, the turbulent atmosphere at home, his relatively poor response to medication, his lack of insight, his antagonism to authority and his hostile aggressive paranoid ideas, especially directed to his wife and family and anyone who disagrees with him, his lack of remorse or guilt with reference to his assaults on his family and his lack of concern for others, I would consider his prognosis to be highly guarded.

The marital disharmony and turbulent home atmosphere would undoubtedly have been caused by the patient's inadequate medical treatment, yet the psychiatrist's words included covert criticism of the wife. He went on:

I would willingly try my best to see this patient settled in the community as soon as possible. It would appear, however, that his home atmosphere has been fraught with tension and conflicts for many years and would be unlikely to change for

113

the better and be far from conducive to his own recovery. He is currently incapable of looking after himself and would need rehabilitation and support beside medical and nursing supervision in order to lead a reasonable, happy and constructive life in society.

This case history is particularly illuminating of the psychiatrist's views. Both the family and the doctor had been at the receiving end of the patient's paranoia and had not liked it, and yet the family was expected to be able to live in peace and harmony with him while he was assaulting them verbally and physically. This family and many others like them are judged to be contributing to disharmony; there seems to be no understanding that it is the patient's paranoia which is the destructive element. These reports contain little sense of compassion for the family and little comprehension of the frightening life they had experienced when living alone with such a severely ill patient.

Exploitation of families

In the *Guardian* of 14 November 1988 Dr Alexander Brown, newly elected chairman of the Royal College of Psychiatrists' Nursing Committee, was quoted as saying: 'There is a national shortage of psychiatric nurses and staff numbers are often below par. We have a greater recruiting problem than in general medicine and an equal problem in retaining staff. It can be a much more stressful job than general nursing.' Now if it is stressful for trained psychiatric nurses, who have time off and shared responsibility, how much more stressful is it for near relatives to care for a schizophrenic, very often for twenty-four hours a day, with no break and no peace of mind? The patient may be delusional, paranoid, angry, aggressive or manic, and perhaps spending any money he can get hold of; or he may be very depressed and suicidal and have to be constantly watched. To live for one day with someone so ill is an agony. When that agony is prolonged for weeks, months or years, under the pretext that the patient is better off in the community, it is time to call a halt.

Harriet Lefley (1987) writes about

the current tendency of the provider system to use families as a first and last resort for difficult patients, without providing any preparation for the caregiving role. Approximately 65 per cent of hospitalised patients are discharged to their families [in the USA] . . . there are remarkably few attempts to offer simple instruction in medication effects and behaviour management to those who need it most . . . we see little evidence of outreach to involve families in treatment and discharge planning, or to solicit their feedback on outpatients' responses to treatment.

Thus the families are still being blamed for producing the illness, and at the same time they are being exploited by being made to act as full-time unpaid nurses.

Cries for help

Families want above all to get the patient well, but if they are pushed to the limits of their endurance their own health and ability to cope decline. When the psychiatrist believes they have contributed to the psychosis the position of the family is precarious, to say the least. How can such a family call for help (assuming that the patient has not cut the telephone cord to start with), knowing that they will probably not be believed? If they do get through, consultant psychiatrists are busy and often highly elusive. Exhausted relatives of paranoid or suicidal patients suffer appallingly at such times.

One SAGB member told me that her son's behaviour was 'bizarre and unpredictable', yet

He manages always to keep within the law. Our appeals for him to be given medication have fallen on deaf ears until he becomes a danger to himself and others. He is living in a broken-down caravan with no proper sanitation or water . . . we have been told by the social workers etc. that we are not to support him in any way, but to let him sink to the bottom and then they can step in.

What do you do when your son turns up at midnight on a cold wet night with no money and nowhere to go? Do you turn him away? We can't do it, and I don't see any caring parents doing it. If this is community care, then God help us. It puts a dreadful burden on families.

If GPs and psychiatrists could but understand the superhuman effort that has to be made by relatives in order to get medical assistance, would they act so callously towards them? Schizophrenia does, after all, run in families, and sometimes the relatives themselves may be suffering from some less severe psychiatric illness. Medical response to cries for help from all families who devote their lives to caring for a schizophrenic patient should be instant and compassionate.

Immediate hospitalization is usually needed, both to stabilize the patient with drugs and to give the family time to recover. In these circumstances a crisis intervention team coming to the home serves no purpose. Far from wanting new disruptions, the family needs peace from their existing ones – they need to be separated from the patient. An hour or two with a team of interfering experts seeking psychological solutions to medical problems is worse than useless. When they have left the house a paranoid patient is likely to be more exhausted and paranoid than ever, and the relatives even more at their wits' end.

Educating the family

It is quite intimidating for families at the best of times when a patient returns home after his first visit to hospital to be treated for schizophrenia. The waiting relatives feel tense. Will their son, or father, still be hostile and angry? Will he be able to go back to work? Will he go to a day centre or to an industrial unit? Will the psychiatrist talk to them about the future? What *is* the future?

For most families there will be few answers, if any, to their questions. They will not be taught to regard schizophrenia as a physical disease, even though this attitude is of vast importance to anyone caring for a schizophrenic. It is essential for the relatives to understand that personality is dependent on brain and body chemistry, and that this can go awry through a disease process.

Human beings have a very limited ability to change their personalities; for someone whose personality has changed through a disease process, this limited ability is diminished still further. One's personality can probably be changed more through diet than through any other means (except drugs), but nutritional expertise is not yet precise enough for this to be achieved effectively. In Chapter 7 I shall talk about present knowledge in this area, but for now it has to be realized that the concept of free will is limited. It is wrong to expect too much from anyone. Once this lesson has been learnt, the behaviour of others – especially the mentally ill – can be viewed more objectively. In caring for a schizophrenic it is necessary to accept all sorts of abnormal behaviour with as much equanimity as possible, however hard the task.

No one can choose his or her genetic endowment, and those with the gene for schizophrenia have been given a harsh hand to play. They need a lot of help, understanding and compassion from their carers and from society; many people in our increasingly hard society seem not to know or care about the mentally ill and their families. We have to learn to accept others as they are, and try to help them rather than to judge them. We have to learn how unwise it is to expect anything from patients: it may be impossible for them to show or to feel love, compassion or kindness when they are ill.

Caring for the carers

If the relatives who care for them are not able to stand back objectively and accept abnormal behaviour for what it is, they too may need medical help because of undergoing prolonged periods of stress and/or from carrying the schizophrenia gene, even if not wholly expressing it. Doctors should look after the relatives of the mentally ill with particular care and insight.

A paper published by the Scottish Schizophrenia Group in 1987 described 'a very high incidence of psychological distress in relatives [of patients who have suffered first attacks of schizophrenia] with anxiety-based symptoms the most prominent feature'. More than 75 per cent of thirty-one main care-giving relatives had 'a high probability of themselves being a psychiatric case. Relatives also showed social role dysfunction and impairment, especially marked in social and leisure activities. Relatives' distress was related to the level of symptoms in patients.'

Emotional levels

Suggestions have been made in recent years that if relatives react to a patient's illness by expressing high emotion (known as high EE – high expressed emotion), the patient may relapse more readily; and that if the patient is given neuroleptic medication and has reduced face-to-face contact with his high EE relative, he is less likely to relapse.

At one conference I attended, after a lecture on emotion in relatives a member of the audience got up to speak. She said she was a high EE mother who could not help reacting to the illness in her family. That woman should have received medical help, and should not have had to make huge efforts to remain calm when it was not in her nature. The fact that she was a high EE mother obviously made her feel in a very inferior position. Was she, even only as a result of hearing that day's lecture, feeling guilty? Was she one of those relatives whose high anxiety level was induced by her schizophrenic relative? Relatives should stay calm if they are able, but should not feel guilty if they cannot. Once again I fear psychiatrists may be blaming relatives whilst expecting them at the same time to be perfect carers.

The two faces of professional advice

The help and education given to relatives should be clear and consistent, but rarely is. Harriet Lefley, writing in 1987, says that 'Families are exposed to a continuous double bind if they read the contradictory literatures on mental illness and their correlative treatment approaches. Messages from professionals caution against rejection and over-involvement, under-stimulation and over-stimulation, over-protection and guarding against premature independence.' Two opposite instructions can produce total confusion in relatives. Lefley describes family therapists 'who use subterfuge whilst emphasising authenticity . . . covert blame of the family by professionals is often combined with overt attempts to help them, while the contradiction is denied.'

I was particularly gratified to read these comments, for they endorse my own feelings that the professionals are often very two-faced to the relatives. However, it is possible to train one's antennae to see through the charm and to detect the blame so often still laid upon the relatives of schizophrenics. Many psychiatrists have no hesitation in revealing their innermost opinions – including blaming the relatives – to the patient. Sadly, the patient usually believes the doctor, for the doctor is seen to be a professional expert.

In an ideal world . . .

So how, in a perfect situation, should a case of schizophrenia be handled? Let us imagine the best kind of case history. The relative recognizes the onset of a schizophrenic illness. The GP and psychiatrist visit the home, and agree that the patient should be hospitalized under the Mental Health Act 1983 for the sake of his health. He goes to hospital, probably under Section 2 (up to twenty-eight days in hospital, which can include compulsory treatment). He makes no fuss, because his illness has been identified early.

When he gets to hospital his psychiatrist teaches him and his family about schizophrenia. The doctor explains that it is an inherited disease which causes alterations in the chemistry of the body and the brain, and that the the patient has to learn all about his disease and co-operate in getting well.

At the same time the psychiatrist will be trying out different medications in succession until he finds one which suits that particular individual. He carefully adjusts the dosage for maximum benefit. He keeps the patient in hospital for a reasonable length of time until he is sure that the symptoms, especially the paranoia and irritability, are well controlled. Only then does he discharge him.

The family is delighted to see the patient home again and in such a good state of mental health, and they all get on with their lives once more. The patient resumes his former job and takes his maintenance medication faithfully.

The doctor has done his work responsibly and the patient has learnt how to keep himself well balanced. He realizes that his symptoms may return if he drinks alcohol, and so he keeps off it. He exercises in the open air and perhaps swims regularly. He eats sensibly. He has few problems and his relatives are delighted.

The hospital psychiatrists and nurses would, I am sure, like this ideal case to be the experience of all patients. Sadly, it is not. Lack of information to both the patient and his family is a frequent and unnecessary situation.

The importance of the 'sick role'

'The Medical Model and the Responsible Patient' is the title of a paper written by American experts Dr Cynthia Bisbee, Dr Humphrey Osmond and Dr Mullaly, who consider schizophrenia and manic depression to be illnesses with a chemical basis. Patients of theirs who suffer from either are told their diagnosis at once; as a result the patients are fully aware that they are suffering from a disease – and a disease which is given its proper name. When they enter Bryce Hospital in Tuscaloosa, Alabama they are given what is called the 'sick role' – in other words, the presence of illness is acknowledged and everyone accepts that the patient is sick. 'The sick role,' say the authors, 'provides a place [a hospital] for those who are too ill to perform their usual functions. It is in theory a temporary role, a place saver and preserving a person's identity until recovery occurs.'

So often in Britain – frequently as a matter of deliberate policy – the schizophrenic patient is not given a diagnosis; he is not told he has a real disease which has altered his normal brain and body chemistry. Without the sick role, he is left in a terrifying vacuum. Additionally, he is still often led to believe that it is his family, or society, which has caused him to feel as he does. The authors of this paper refer to *The Social System*, a book written in 1951 by Talcott Parsons, who says that

sick people have the right to blamelessness for being ill and the right to an appropriate reduction of their normal obligations. In exchange for these rights, patients must accept certain duties. They must first try to get well as quickly as possible and must cooperate with those who have the social responsibility to help in their recovery such as doctors, nurses and other helping people . . . responsible patients must cooperate if they want to fill their role properly.

Dr Osmond and his colleagues say that in about 1970 the idea of the sick role was allowed to lapse for a time at Bryce Hospital, 'because of the prevalent belief that to consider oneself sick was to cease to be responsible for one's actions'. We all know that to expect someone with a bad attack of flu to go out to work would be to deny him the sick role and deprive him of his need to be given hot water bottles and be generally fussed over: we would not expect a flu sufferer to perform his normal role in society. However, very ill schizophrenic patients are constantly being told by psychiatrists that they are merely lazy; they are told to look for work in open competition with well people, and are totally denied their sick role. Here is an account by the mother of a young woman, ill in hospital with schizophrenia, who is clearly denied the sick role:

She drops food and drink all over her clothes and gets told to wash them again, even when she has only just put them on. She is told when to do her washing but she is too ill to do it properly. She is on Largactil, Modecate injections, Stelazine, pills to stop the shakes from the drugs, and pills because she goes berserk when she has a period. If she falls asleep during the day she is curtly told to wake up because she won't sleep at night. But, as you can imagine, she finds it nearly impossible to keep awake at all. The only happy thing she can think of is that God has sent her a message that she can die within a year. That is the only thing that cheers her up.

Dr Osmond and his colleagues say: 'There is now evidence that [psychiatric] patients do better, get well faster and stay well if they are given the sick role, that is, if they understand that they are ill and that they must participate in treatment. They are no longer considered irresponsible if they call themselves ill.'

Educating the patient

Patients admitted to Bryce Hospital are 'assigned to a responsible patient class in which they are taught the rights and obligations of responsible patients to know about the illness; to participate in treatment planning and to follow treatment routines'. They attend five thirty-five-minute classes a day on four consecutive days, starting with

> an orientation class which is an introduction to the salient features of hospitalisation, such as evaluation procedures, treatment services available, and discharge procedures. Other core classes include those on health and medication, community resources, family dynamics and learning to live effectively. The last is a class in the daily emotional routines of living such as dealing with feelings; seeing various points of view and learning to plan and solve problems . . . The intention is to be explicit and to provide useful information about mental illness in a clear simple manner . . .
>
> Patients are taught that in mental illness, as in diabetes, real physical and chemical changes occur. The goal of treatment is to control the effects of these changes and to restore hope for a relatively normal life.
>
> Patients also learn that in mental illnesses, changes in neurochemistry lead to changes in the senses, in the perception of the self and others, in thought, feelings and actions and in everyday life. Patients are taught that they are not responsible for the chemical changes but they are responsible for their effects and for taking the necessary steps to control the effects.

If such honesty and openness were the norm towards all schizophrenic patients, and if compassion were the order of the day instead of blame and punishment – whether to patients or relatives – it would be much easier to help patients when they were sent home.

Dr Osmond continues:

> Patients learn that they occupy an esteemed role of responsible patient with special rights, duties and social status. As a

responsible patient, each has the right to safety and security, the right to decreased stress whilst ill, the right to be placed in the responsible patient role and not in unacceptable roles such as 'bad' or 'crazy'; the right to information about diagnoses and treatment, the right to medical and dental care and the right to adequate treatment for mental illness, including a full treatment plan and realistic discharge plans.

The duties of the responsible patient are also outlined. He must know he is ill, when and how he is ill and what to do about the illness. He must also act responsibly and not bad or crazy, work with the doctors and the treatment team and play his part in getting well. Patients learn that there are several unacceptable roles such as being 'a nothing', 'bad' or 'crazy'. All these roles are shown to involve a significant reduction in rights, responsibility and social status, leading to misunderstanding, social problems and failure to receive proper treatment.

I presume what is meant here is that if a patient has any control over his own actions he must exercise severe self-discipline to prevent himself from acting in such a way as to alienate society. But this is not an easy role for a severely ill psychiatric patient; some may find it impossible. With medical treatment self-discipline becomes less of a problem, but it is rarely as easy for the psychiatric patient to behave in a socially acceptable manner as it is for those with no such disease.

The paper continues:

The objective of the third class [in the series] is to deal with the concept of treatment and how the patient can best participate in his own treatment programme. The neurochemical model of changing perceptions, thoughts, feelings, actions and everyday life is reviewed to explain how the patient is to control these changes – that is, to get well quickly and to live within his limit and to stay well most of the time, using the assistance of his doctor and his prescribed medicine.

Patients learn the requirements of the medical plan; to ask the doctor for help, to show trust in the doctor, to listen to the doctor's plan and to come up with a joint plan to know more about the prescribed medication – what it is, why it is needed, what effects may appear.

Patients also learn that as part of the full treatment they are expected to learn more about their general health (cleanliness, diet, health-care and medication for physical illness), their recreations and their own special problems in dealing with family and community. Emphasis is placed on continuing the medical treatment plan as well as dealing effectively with special problems such as stress, rest and exercise, alcohol and drug abuse. It is emphasised that only as a responsible patient can one fully participate in the struggle against illness and thus become a respected member of society.

I have quoted at length from his paper because it shows what can be done for a patient in hospital before he returns to his family. Honesty in discussing problems, symptoms and medication helps him tremendously. If he has an educational programme like this to fall back on it will stand him and his family in good stead. The work of Dr Osmond and his colleagues at Bryce Hospital is an inspiration; if his precepts were followed widely by all our psychiatrists, there would be a quiet revolution.

Poor aftercare in Britain

This American paper was published in 1980; but in the interim – at least in Britain – things have gone from bad to worse. Seeking to explore how the policy of running down and closing psychiatric hospitals was affecting the well-being of patients, Dr Johnstone (1984) and her colleagues at the Clinical Research Centre, Harrow, Middlesex, traced sixty-six patients who had been discharged from Shenley Hospital (Herts) between 1970 and 1974. During the year before the interviews fifty-five of these patients had not seen a psychiatrist, and fifty-one of their families had had no contact with a social worker. Over half the patients were clearly psychotic and were severely impaired all the time. Their relatives were distressed 'at the patients' obvious suffering, dependence, loneliness, apathy, slowness and fear of relapse or deterioration'.

Some of the symptoms just mentioned are negative ones. While paranoid schizophrenia is more prevalent, and has more violent and frightening symptoms, negative symptoms – which can be most distressing to both patient and family – should not be ignored. Professor J. H. Wing (1987) described the effects:

A severely affected individual is slow to think and move, speaks little, has little energy and appears apathetic. The non-verbal as well as the verbal means of communication are often affected. Speech, and therefore thought, is often muddled to the point of incoherence. Other people find little reward in such company and the individual may be miserably aware of loneliness but have no ability to overcome it.

The relatives in Johnstone's study 'expressed the view that the staff of the psychiatric services were ill-equipped to deal with patients in whom recovery was not taking place. The chronicity of illness shown [in this study] highlights the need for developing community services to take account of the fact that there is a substantial proportion of the schizophrenic population in whom, with available methods of treatment, recovery is not going to take place and that many of these patients need a high degree of care . . . this care was provided by relatives who were in many cases frail, ageing and coping only with great difficulty.'

Three examples were given of the sort of lives led by these patients and their families. The first patient was a fifty-year-old man, living with his seventy-one-year-old mother. He was attending a psychiatric clinic, and had gone to a day centre for many years. The patient was described as very dependent upon his mother for most aspects of his life, and had no friends or social contacts. When he was interviewed, he appeared unkempt and rather dirty. He scored the maximum number of points on hallucinations and thought disorder; he was probably deluded, too, but he was so incoherent that this could not be clearly determined.

The second patient, a twenty-seven-year-old woman living with her sixty-one-year-old widowed father, was receiving no medical or social support. She did not work and never went out without her father. She was verbally and physically aggressive towards him, and at times damaged the furniture and other items in the home. She could make no attempt at personal cleanliness, and was at times incontinent. Her father was much troubled by the unsuitability of his dealing with her personal hygiene. When she was interviewed, she adopted bizarre postures and her behaviour was very degraded. She showed gross mood disorder and her speech was very unintelligible, and, although she would not discuss them, she alluded to hallucinations and delusions.

The third patient was a fifty-eight-year-old housewife, living with her husband and twenty-two-year-old son. She too was receiving no medical or social suport. Believing that her family were poisoning her, she shopped and cooked for herself alone and would not remain in the same room with them. She shouted at night to hallucinations, and was abusive to any visitor who called. At her interview she would not reply to any of the questions. She was dressed in a bizarre way and was surrounded by items which apeared to have symbolic significance. Affective incongruity was gross, and her laconic remarks were not entirely coherent.

In brief such people, be they patients or relatives, cannot cope. Dr Johnstone's study reveals graphically that patients were being grossly neglected by doctors and social workers, whether for policy reasons or because they were overstretched. The medical and social services should have been keeping a watchful eye on these discharged patients, many of whom should have been taken back into hospital for a more vigorous and scientific approach to their treatment.

For patients and their families, coping does not mean living properly: it means managing as best they can in intolerable circumstances. What is more, a whole new concept is arising, that of helping people to cope and seeing how they do cope.

The concept of coping

In 1987 Tarrier published the findings of his investigation into the residual psychotic symptoms of discharged schizophrenic patients. He examined twenty-five people who had been discharged from hospital while still experiencing hallucinations and/or delusions. Instead of being returned to hospital to see if their medication could be adjusted, the patients were interviewed about their

symptoms and asked how they coped with them. The following were mentioned:
- Thinking of another subject (other, presumably, than being dictated to by their voices)
- Trying to think of nothing
- Telling themselves their thoughts were not real but part of their illness
- Playing loud music
- Attempting to relax
- Drinking alcohol

Of twenty-five patients, seventeen experienced true hallucinations, two experienced pseudo-hallucinations (which are perhaps transitory, and may be caused by sensory deprivation), and nineteen experienced delusions. The author concludes that:

> It may be that any psychological interventions would be suitable only for patients who had improved sufficiently on neuroleptic medication to be able to recognise their illness and identify symptoms, and that attempts to question patients during their acute phase were abandoned due to the frequent delusional nature of their responses . . . Given that residual symptoms in discharged patients are both distressing and disabling, the identification of the determinants of these symptoms with a view to instigating programmes to train patients in appropriate and effective coping skills is a viable possibility.

It may be that patients could and should be taught how to deal with minor residual symptoms, but it would seem an impossible task to suggest mechanisms for dealing with the florid symptoms of schizophrenia, and cruel to suggest strategies which could only produce minor alleviations of these severe symptoms. Tarrier recognizes this, yet nowhere does he suggest what seems obvious to me – that the majority of patients in this study should have been returned to hospital for a reassessment of their medication. Imagine the plight of a family trying to cope with a schizophrenic relative coping with his voice by playing loud music incessantly. Many undoubtedly do learn to bear with it, but it is not the answer to the problem.

It is horrifying to think that so many patients exhibiting delusions and hallucinations are commonly discharged from hospital in this condition. However, in mitigation it must be admitted that some patients do not tell their doctors their symptoms when they are in hospital, since they are so anxious to be discharged. Doctors should be aware of these possibilities and avoid hasty discharge. As one patient said to me: 'If they'd known what I was thinking when they discharged me from hospital, they wouldn't have let me out!'

When patients are discharged home still symptomatic they should always be treated as the ill people they are. They should be given regular meals with good nourishing food. Sleep should be more than adequate as often people with schizophrenia feel very exhausted. Symptoms increase as exhaustion increases. The patient should go to bed early so that he can relax and perhaps read in bed. Always be kind and compassionate to the patient, remembering always that his behavioural symptoms, if present, are DISEASE SYMPTOMS. Try not to react to paranoia and anger. Love and kindness, good food and lots of rest and sleep can help the patient, but good medicating by the psychiatrist is of major importance. If symptoms persist these should be reported in detail to the doctor. It may be easier to write a letter, as letters are clearer and points can be made as they occur. Even if the doctor does not reply the information is useful to him and can probably lead to his understanding his patients better and to an improvement in his ability to medicate well.

The patient should never go hungry or his blood sugar may drop and at such times his symptoms will increase.

The patient should never get over-tired, or his symptoms will increase. He needs peace and quietness and a great deal of rest as well as adequate, but not too much, exercise.

Summary of main points

● It is essential that patients should not be discharged until they have lost their major symptoms.
● Politicians and health authorities must be made aware of the great need to keep all our psychiatric hospitals. Patients and their families need the protection of the hospitals.
● It is better for discharged patients not to be housebound and isolated, but either to return to their former job, or, if that is

not possible, perhaps to attend day hospitals or day centres run by voluntary organizations, if they enjoy doing so.
● For far too long relatives and patients have been kept in the dark about schizophrenia, and efforts must be made now to reverse this.
● Most patients are eager to find out all they can about their illness, but will rarely accept information from a relative; they have more faith in their doctor, for he is seen as an expert professional.
● Alcohol and street drugs worsen schizophrenia; the doctor should tell patients about this.
● Smoking may have the same effect, but it is hard to ask a patient to give up what may be his sole source of pleasure.

References

BISBEE, C.; OSMOND, H., MULLALY, (1980): The Medical Model and the Responsible Patient.

JOHNSTONE, E. C., et al: 'Schizophrenic patients discharged from hospital: a follow-up study'. *Brit. J. Psych.* 145, 586-90. Macmillan, 1984.

LEFLEY, HARRIET P. (1987): *'The Family's Response to Mental Illness in a Relative*, in 'Families of the Mentally Ill: Meeting the Challenge'. ed. A. B. Hatfield; San Francisco. Josey-Bass.

MINAS, I. H.; JOSHUA, S. D., JACKSON, H. J. & BURGESS, P. H. (1988): 'Persistent Psychotic Symptoms at Discharge in Patients with Schizophrenia.' *Australian & N. Zealand J. of Psychiatry* 22: 166-172.

PARSONS, TALCOTT (1951): 'The Social System'. Free Press. Glencoe. Illinois.

REIBEL, S.; HERZ, M. I. (1976): 'Limitations of brief hospital treatment'. *American J. of Psychiatry*, 133: 518-21.

THE SCOTTISH SCHIZOPHRENIA RESEARCH GROUP (1987): 'Scottish First Episode Schizophrenia Study IV: Psychiatric and social impact on relatives.' *Brit. J. Psych.* 15: 340–4.

TARRIER, N., (1987): 'An Investigation of Residual Pyschotic Symptoms in Discharged Schizophrenic Patients.' *Brit. J. of Clin. Psychiatry* 26: 141-43.

WING, J. K. (1987) 'Reasoning about Modules? – Public Policy on Severe Mental Disorders.' *R.S.M. Journal*, January 1988.

7

DIET, DRINK, DRUGS AND SMOKING

Old theories rejected

'It seems to me,' wrote the famous French psychiatrist Pinel in 1807, 'that the primary seat of insanity generally is in the region of the stomach and intestines.' Even earlier, in 1631, Burton had slated the humble cabbage for the same reason: 'It causeth troublesome dreams and sends up black vapours to the brain,' he wrote, continuing: 'All pulses are naught, beans, peas, vetches, etc. they fill the brain . . . with gross fumes, breed black thick blood, and cause troublesome dreams'! Such views have, however, been generally discredited nowadays, and the idea that food may produce psychotic disease in the presence of a faulty gene is anathema to most psychiatrists, who regard it as unorthodox, unscientific and 'alternative'.

We are what we eat

But the food we eat and the air we breathe are made up of chemicals, and they interact with our body chemicals to make us what we are. Surely it is wrong to investigate faulty body chemistry without taking into account what the patient eats and drinks? Without food, people die. With the wrong food or the wrong balance of nutrients, they may develop disease. If a person is born with a genetic defect it is particularly important to find out which foods put the most stress on it and which the least, so that the diet can be adjusted.

No firm conclusions yet for schizophrenics

The onset of chronic disease, such as schizophrenia, is gradual, like a river silting up. The American expert Dr F. Curtis Dohan believes that it is the eating of certain foods over a long period of time which produces schizophrenia in those with the genetic propensity to do so, and that the reversing of this disease process takes an equally long period. But at the present time nothing is known for certain about the effects of treating schizophrenia through diet, and we human beings are impatient creatures, even when we are well. It would be extremely difficult for a schizophrenic patient to come to terms with this and say: 'I am irrational, angry and uncommunicative possibly because I have eaten bread and drunk milk for the first twenty years of my life. Now I must give them both up for a year on the off chance that I may recover my mental health.'

Sadly, no firm conclusions have yet been drawn on the subject of diet for schizophrenics. I believe that the disease *will* prove to be treatable by diet, but in the meantime we can say no more than that the experts are still experimenting. There are, however, some obvious avenues to explore and some sensible guidelines to follow, which appear later in the chapter.

Effects of food and drink on mentally healthy people

Before considering diet in relation to schizophrenia it would be useful to discuss the effects of diet on those whom society considers normal. We all know that excessive alcohol affects thought, mood and behaviour. Some people may become unconscious, whilst others may become aggressive and violent. Tea and coffee may make people unduly anxious because of their caffeine content. A bedtime snack containing cheese may cause nightmares, and heavy foods such as pastry and suet pudding at lunchtime may make people fall asleep in the middle of the afternoon.

Compatibility of food and metabolism

All animals need vitamins and minerals in order to thrive. These nutrients enable enzymes (substances which speed up chemical changes in the body) to function effectively. Proteins, carbohydrates and fats are essential components in our diet; the problem is getting the balance right. The medical profession today is awakening to the fact that what people eat may produce disease if it is the wrong sort of food for a certain metabolism.

The benefits of starvation for schizophrenics

In 1971 the SAGB heard from Dr A. Cutt about the pioneering work done in Moscow by Professor Nicolayev, who treated his psychiatric patients by starving them of all food for a period of twenty to thirty days; they had to drink at least a litre of water each day. Strict hospital conditions were essential, because a starvation diet of this kind can be very dangerous and must only ever be undertaken with close medical supervision.

During the recovery period Nicolayev began reintroducing food gradually, starting with fruit juice, going on to grated apple, yoghurt, oranges and raw carrots, and then continuing with a complete vegetable diet. On the sixth day after the fast had ended small amounts of cottage cheese were being eaten, together with honey and brown bread. No meat was allowed for six months, and then only in very small quantities; a diet without meat, eggs or fish was preferred. Apparently paranoid schizophrenics did very well during the fasting period, but their improvement was reversed once they started eating again. Since 64 per cent of Nicolayev's schizophrenic patients lost their symptoms while fasting it would be justifiable to think that food had contributed to their symptoms.

Dr Dohan received a letter from Professor Anastasopoulas, a psychiatrist from Athens, in which he noted that in Greece during the Second World War lack of food had had a beneficial effect on schizophrenic patients. He wrote that 'schizophrenics became almost sane during the last days before they died in the starvation period . . . the worst period was in 1941 under the Nazi occupation . . . bread, a basic food for Greeks, was for many months non-existent, and the patients were living on one egg and one herring a day. It must be noted moreover that schizophrenics had a good survival capacity.'

Mental illness rates in the first and third worlds

Dr Dohan (1966) said that in certain parts of the world people appear to be much freer from mental illness than they are in the West. He quoted studies of native tribes carried out in Taiwan, Kenya and Ghana, and said that it was generally recognized that the adoption of Western culture, including food habits, was associated with an increase in mental illness. Many children of West Indian immigrants to the U.K. have to be sent to hospital for schizophrenia treatment. Could it be that the original immigrants have stuck with their old culture and eating habits, while their children have had to adopt Western diet at school or in the workplace? If so, the new diet may have precipitated mental breakdowns that would not have occurred had they eaten the food to which their parents were accustomed. If this hypothesis turns out to be true, the effects could be very far-reaching: it would be tragic if, in our concern to feed those nations who are hungrier and less privileged than the affluent West, we ended up driving them mad.

The suspects: wheat and milk

Efforts by the West to feed milk and wheat products to third world countries sometimes meet with opposition due to a self-protective aversion to foods which may be felt to cause harm. One researcher reported that workers involved in a certain village construction project in Bangladesh were paid in wheat, but were very reluctant to take it instead of their familiar rice, without which they thought they would die.

Dried milk created even more problems. Milk was an uncommon food after infancy here, as in other parts of Asia and in West Africa and Latin America; children to whom it was given complained of diarrhoea and stomach ache. One researcher, Dr W. Philpott, reported that 70 per cent of coloured people were deficient in lactase, the enzyme that breaks down lactose (milk sugar) in the gut. Such people, if given milk to drink, may become deficient in calcium and magnesium. In Chapter 2 many schizophrenic members of the SAGB reported how sensitive to milk they had been when young.

Dr Philpott found that half his sample of schizophrenic patients were unable to drink milk for one of three reasons. Some were allergic to it; others had a lactase deficiency; and yet others could not convert the milk sugar, galactose, to glycogen, leading to a build-up of toxic substances. Apart from problems with milk, Dr Philpott found that 64 per cent of his patients were wheat-sensitive.

Dr Dohan wrote: 'The kinds of cereal from products customarily eaten may be a major factor in the production of psychiatric symptoms in those with susceptibility to schizophrenia', and bases this hypothesis on three observations. First, during the Second World War changes in numbers admitted to hospital for first-time schizophrenia treatment tied in with changes in wheat and rye consumption as a result of shortages. First admissions of women for schizophrenia varied from a decrease of 45% in the second three war years in Finland to plus 15% in the same period in the USA. Variations in cereal consumption (wheat and rye) were comparable as grain imports were drastically reduced in Finland during the war. Second, schizophrenia and coeliac disease occur in the same person more frequently than would be expected by chance. Wheat gluten (a mixture of proteins) and similar proteins in other cereals produce coeliac disease in those with an inherited susceptibility to it. Since both diseases are inherited, Dohan suggests that they may share one or more faulty genes. Third, a group of relapsed schizophrenics given a milk- and cereal-free diet improved almost twice as fast as those on a high-cereal diet, but the milk- and cereal-free patients fell back when wheat gluten was secretly added to their diet.

Dohan says that the geographical incidence of schizophrenia varies with the kind of cereal grains eaten. Wheat- and rye-producing areas have the highest incidence of the disease. Oats and barley come next, followed by rice areas, which have about 60 per cent of the incidence in the wheat-growing areas. In sorghum and maize areas the incidence is only about 25 per cent of that in the wheat areas, while in the Highlands of New Guinea, where hardly any grain is eaten, there is practically no schizophrenia at all.

Do some peptides cause hallucinations?

Amino-acids are known as the building blocks of protein. Peptides are small lengths of protein containing only a few amino-acids. Many peptides are formed as a result of the digestion of protein in the gut.

In coeliac disease, peptides derived from wheat are thought to be the cause of damage to the lining of the small intestine. When the finger-like villi are destroyed they leave a much smaller area for the absorption of nutrients from the small intestine into the blood. In Chapter 3 the Italian researcher Dr Buscaino was reported as having found gut damage in unmedicated schizophrenics similar to that found in sufferers from coeliac disease. Was this damage, too, caused by harmful peptides derived from wheat proteins and milk? Does the genetic fault in schizophrenia involve an enzyme, which, if in short supply, would fail to break down certain proteins in a normal way, leading to the production of abnormal peptides – as is thought to be the case in coeliac disease? Do such hypothetical abnormal peptides directly affect the brain? Dr Christine Zioudrou has found that certain peptides derived from milk and grains have similar effects to those produced by opium. Do these opioid-like peptides go to the brain of schizophrenics in greater than normal quantities, and perhaps contribute to hallucinations? Do schizophrenics undergo the heroin experience without taking heroin?

The 'thinking' body

Richard Bergland (1985) has some very interesting ideas about peptides which act as hormones and transmitters in the brain. He regards the brain as a gland which secretes many peptide hormones which are transmitters, and believes that varied regulatory hormones, which are the stuff of the brain, are found all over the body as well as in the brain. In his view, 'thinking' may go on outside as well as inside the brain, and these hormones modulate every aspect of thought and behaviour: they can determine pleasure, love, appetite, joy, sleep, pain, memory, sexual feelings, digestion, sadness, anxiety and so on.

Dr Bergland thinks that these peptide hormones work together in groups, and that in principle certain brain diseases, such as schizophrenia and Alzheimer's disease, may be treatable by hormone replacement as simply as diabetes is now treated with insulin. He suggests that if a canula (narrow tube) were placed in the brain ventricles and a sample of ventricular fluid analysed, any abnormally low peptide level could be discovered and then boosted through a canula. Bergland thinks that brain ventricular fluid is not just there as a cushion for the brain, but that it is the reservoir of peptides for the nourishment of the brain. He believes that it may eventually be possible to treat both Alzheimer's disease and schizophrenia in this way.

'Molecules which you eat and drink and are released when you laugh or cry or exercise,' writes Dr Bergland, 'are released into your brain all the time.' In other words, if food-derived peptides are released which are harmful to the brain, they may produce schizophrenic symptoms in those who are genetically vulnerable by moving upwards through the nerves to the brain. 'Hormones determine all brain/body and brain/behaviour relationships,' he sums up.

> We must acknowledge the unity of the brain and the body . . . The same hormonal codes that flow from the brain to the glands of the body also flow in the reverse direction from the glands to the brain . . . shrinkage of the left cerebellum (part of the brain) occurs if the right testicle is removed and conversely if the left cerebellum is damaged the right testicle is smaller. If the right glands are removed, there are shrunken brain cells on the left. The brain thinks differently if the gonads are removed.

This is interesting as far as schizophrenia is concerned. Before modern drug treatments were available, the glands of the body –

such as the testes and adrenals – were often found to be atrophied. Dr Brooksbank, an MRC researcher, recently told me that in the past hypogonadism (poor functioning gonads) was quite often found in male paranoid schizophrenics.

Studies of peptides common to gut and brain, and those derived from food, will be an important part of the work the Schizophrenia Association of Great Britain is initiating and supporting in the Department of Biochemistry in the University of Wales in Bangor. It is a very exciting field to explore and the interplay of the natural existing peptides which function as hormones and transmitters must surely be affected by the foods we eat.

Digestive problems in schizophrenic adults

In Chapter 2 I talked about digestive problems experienced by schizophrenic SAGB members during infancy and childhood. They were also asked about chronic problems encountered in adulthood, and 108 out of 253 returned questionnaires reported digestive difficulty at some stage in life. Here is a consensus of the replies. The most frequent problems, mentioned in at least three questionnaires and given here starting with the commonest, were:

● Indigestion and nervous dyspepsia (often said to be due to tension)
● Constipation (often said to be due to tension)
● Vomiting
● Diarrhoea
● Wind and flatulence
● Loss of appetite, and general faddiness
● Nausea (sometimes with headache)

General problems with food included:

● Baulks at food and feels sick while eating
● Unable to swallow food
● Severe food allergies
● Very tired after food

137

Some members mentioned problems with particular foods:

- Cannot eat fatty foods
- Cannot eat very rich foods
- Cannot tolerate alcohol
- Craving for sweet foods

General digestive complaints included:

- Swollen stomach
- Stomach upsets leading to loss of consciousness
- Stomach pains
- Pains in lower abdomen
- Travel sickness
- Underweight

Specific diagnosed ailments included:

- Acute gastritis
- Gastric ulcer
- Duodenal ulcer
- Serious liver complaint
- Colitis
- Renal colic
- Undulant fever (a recurring fever similar to brucellosis in cattle, but less severe)

Effective cures mentioned included:

- Giving up smoking
- Following a gluten-free diet
- Eating yoghurt and vitamin B12 (one reply said that the whole family appeared to suffer from a shortage of B12)

Investigations that had revealed nothing untoward, despite the fact that the patients experienced some of the worst symptoms listed above, included:

- Barium meal
- X-ray for apparent blockage of oesophagus.

Vitamins, minerals and mental health

One mother wrote to me about the effects of vitamins on her schizophrenic son's health:

> He has an injection of Depixol every three weeks. This keeps him stable, except for bad heads with voices which were occurring at least once a day, so that he was afraid to venture far from home and wouldn't go on holiday. He said he felt safe at home. A few months ago he heard that vitamin B might be of help, so he brought home Brewer's Yeast tablets. Almost immediately his bad heads came less frequently – it was unbelievable. He now has one only occasionally – perhaps just once a week, and then only slight. He has also been on holiday with me with no ill effects. There has been no other alteration in his diet, or anything else to account for the change. It is a wonderful relief to both of us.

The possible relationship between schizophrenia and coeliac disease, described earlier in this chapter, suggests that some untreated schizophrenics may be short of various vitamins and minerals because the damaged gut cannot let enough of them pass through into the bloodstream. The story above would certainly suggest this possibility. Vitamins and minerals are vital for the proper working of enzymes in the body and the absence of even one essential nutrient may have devastating mental effects. Many near relatives of schizophrenics suffer from pernicious anaemia, and a deficiency of B12 should always be tested for in patients.

Research undertaken by Dr Carney of Northwick Park Hospital has indeed revealed that many psychiatric patients, including schizophrenics, are low in vitamin B12 or folic acid. Sourkes (1962) says that 'subjects with low vitamin B12 levels are unable to metabolise a test load of tyrosine effectively and a transamination product of this amino acid, p-hydroxyphenyl pyriuvic acid is readily detectable in large amounts in serum and urine.'

This might be a useful test for all schizophrenic patients. Another pointer to an inability to metabolize tyrosine are changes in pigmentation – patients may develop unpigmented patches of skin (vitiligo) and lose their hair colour or they may go to the other extreme and develop areas of bronze pigmentation.

Derivatives of folic acid assist in the conversion of tyrosine to dopa, and B12 is needed to convert noradrenalin to adrenalin. Since the genetic defect that gives rise to schizophrenia may lie in one of the enzymes involved in this area of metabolism, it is surely important to ensure that enough of all the other necessary nutrients is present.

Dr Chris Reading (1984) says that low levels of vitamins B12, B3, B1 and folic acid, or an under-active thyroid, are often associated with severe allergies (I prefer the word 'sensitivities') to milk and grain.

Counter-arguments

The National Institute of Mental Health believes that large doses of vitamins do not significantly improve schizophrenia treatment. They also counsel caution since some vitamins may have detrimental side effects when taken in large quantities. 'Reliance on high-dose vitamins as a treatment for schizophrenia,' it says in one of its leaflets, 'is not scientifically justified and does have risks.'

Yet, as has been shown, psychiatric patients are sometimes low in certain vitamins, and such deficiencies are known to cause psychiatric symptoms. Where deficiencies are found, they should be made good.

Elements

Our bodies need calcium, magnesium, phosphorus and other elements in large amounts for structural purposes; while minute quantities of others (known as trace elements, and including lithium, iron, zinc, iodine, copper, chromium, selenium, manganese, molybdenum and cobalt) are necessary to enable enzymes to function properly. Sodium, potassium and chlorine are required to maintain the salt or water balance in the body. Apart from its structural uses, magnesium is needed for the action of many enzymes concerned in the metabolism of carbohydrates. Animals deprived of magnesium are nervous and move unsteadily. The late Dr Carl C. Pfeiffer (1978) has done much work on nutrient deficiencies and excesses in psychiatric patients. He says that 'under stress, when patients lose both zinc and pyridoxine, a characteristic psychosis may develop', and adds that behaviour patterns are closely linked to the network of trace elements – an excess of just one can distort the whole metabolism. He divides the agents that may cause abnormal behaviour into six groups:

● Bacterial toxins and fevers
● Plants such as cannabis, cocoa leaves and psylocybin
● Drugs such as cocaine and cannabinols
● Solvents such as alcohol, carbon tetrachloride, formaldehyde and trichlorethylene
● Metal excesses (e.g. copper, lead, bismuth, mercury and aluminium)
● Metal deficiencies (.e.g. zinc, selenium, manganese, magnesium and molybdenum)

It has already been shown in earlier chapters that schizophrenia is made worse by viral infection, street drugs and alcohol. It would be wise for doctors to consider the levels of all nutrients, whether elements or vitamins, for any effects they might have on mental illness.

Dr J. L. Crammer talked about Trace Metals in Mental Illness at an SAGB conference in 1985, saying that the possibility that a deficiency or an excess of a metal might play a part in the causation of mental illness has received very little consideration. He mentioned the inherited Wilson's disease, which is due to excessive copper, and spoke of lead, manganese and vanadium mining, where workers are exposed to high levels of these elements. The possible toxic effects of lead in petrol fumes were also mentioned, as were those of excess aluminium which may be the cause of pre-senile dementia, known as Alzheimer's disease.

As long ago as 1970 the World Health Organization acknowledged the importance of studying nutrient levels of schizophrenics, and the following year the *Annual Review of Biochemistry* published an article which included these words: 'Human disease in all instances has a biochemical basis, or is accompanied by biochemical alterations. To discover and measure the extent of these alterations as a guide to concise diagnosis and therapy is the central function of the clinical laboratory.' The tide is turning, but it is taking a long time for the ideas to filter through to the research laboratories.

Low blood sugar (hypoglycaemia) and the nervous system

An editorial in the *Lancet* of 5 October 1985 pointed out that the central nervous system's only source of energy derives from the oxidative metabolism of glucose, which makes it very vulnerable to extreme changes in the glucose supply:

> If the glucose supply is cut off CNS function deteriorates rapidly, ultimately leading to irreversible damage . . . the initial symptoms are due to an excessive adrenergic activity [the release of adrenalin] – the patient is tremulous, anxious, sweats profusely and has palpitations. Cerebral dysfunction follows, with alterations in behaviour, especially slowness and irritability, preceding clouding of consciousness and coma. Function may be restored by intravenous glucose.

Drs Abrahamson and Pezet (1971) say that 'it is the balance between the hormone insulin, produced by the pancreas, and the adrenal cortical hormones that keeps the blood sugar at a normal level.' In diabetes, which is often found in the families of schizophrenics, insulin deficiency leads to high levels of sugar in the blood. The treatment consists of insulin injections; but an overdose will reduce the blood sugar too much and result in an insulin coma, because the brain is being starved of its essential glucose. Hypoglycaemia is the reverse of diabetes: the pancreas secretes too much insulin, leaving too little sugar in the blood, thus depriving the brain of its essential nutrient.

'If blood sugar is not properly controlled, the patient may be pale, cold and clammy and have a temperature below normal,' say Abrahamson and Pezet. 'If a meal is delayed the symptoms may become more noticeable and are worse if there is a concurrent infection.' In an unpublished paper Dr J. V. du Plessis and Dr W. H. Davies describe the symptoms like this: 'Any lack of appropriate facial colour indicates problems with the adrenals and/or pituitary and/or pineal glands; bad posture, indistinct speech, poor hearing, flat body language.' They also list the following as being possible symptoms exhibited by people with low blood sugar:

- Accidents
- Premature ageing
- Alcoholism
- Lack of balance
- Belligerence
- Blackouts
- Problems after childbirth
- Collapse
- Poor concentration
- Loss of consciousness
- Craving for sweet things
- Craziness
- Not understanding what they are doing or have done
- Dropping out
- Fatigue
- Flatulence
- Frigidity
- Germ-caused diseases
- Headaches
- Impotence
- Indecision
- Irritability
- Poor memory
- Muddling things
- Rebelliousness
- Generally run-down state
- Lack of sex drive

- Quick temper
- Tiredness
- Vertigo
- Excessive worrying

This extremely long list of possible symptoms of hypoglycaemia has much in common with the symptoms of schizophrenia. Hungry schizophrenics very often become quite desperate for food and exhibit many of their symptoms, behaving in a silly or angry way and appearing to lose touch with reality. 'I'm hungry. I'm almost homicidal,' said the young man whose case history was described in Chapter 1. Dr Davies suggests that schizophrenia is preceded by hypoglycaemia, and that it is necessary to treat all schizophrenics for this condition. Food is always the number one treatment, given with all possible speed.

Essential fatty acids

In the *Lancet* (1979) Dr David Horrobin gave evidence that prostaglandins of the E1 series are deficient in schizophrenia. Prostaglandins are synthesised in the body from essential fatty acids from food. The 1 series of prostaglandins are formed from dihomogammalinolenic acid. Evening primrose oil, borage and blackcurrant seeds are high in this substance. Providing an appropriate supplement from one of these sources may be beneficial in improving memory.

Dr K. S. Vaddadi et al (in press) found that evening primrose oil 'produced a highly significant improvement in total psycho pathology scores and a significant improvement in memory.' Vaddadi found that certain series of essential fatty acids in red cell membrane phospholipids were lower in schizophrenics than in controls. Therefore it seems that other membranes in the body are affected as well as gut membranes in schizophrenia.

Addictions

Some addictions may have a bearing on the nutritional and biochemical state of the patient.

Alcohol

As stated earlier, schizophrenics are advised to leave alcohol well alone. Just a small amount can increase the aggression and violence manifested by paranoid patients. Some researchers have found that both schizophrenics and alcoholics have low levels of an enzyme called monoamine oxidase in blood platelets, but no conclusion has been drawn since the findings are not consistent enough.

Smoking

In the general public, smoking is now declining as a result of health awareness, but amongst schizophrenics it is still a very popular habit – possibly for very good reasons. There is evidence that noradrenaline – known colloquially as the pleasure hormone – is released in the body by nicotine. If smoking gives pleasure to those who may, because of schizophrenia, rarely feel happiness, is it fair to deny this to them? If it were possible to improve the biochemistry of the patient, of course, he might be able to produce enough noradrenaline to feel pleasure without smoking.

Some researchers also believe that smoking may alleviate stress as a result of nicotine's action on pituitary adrenocortical function. If smoking both causes pleasure and relieves stress, those are two very real reasons why so many schizophrenics become heavy smokers.

However, cigarette smoking seems to spoil the appetite, and smokers may not eat enough to keep themselves well nourished. The habit may, therefore, cause an already malnourished patient to reduce his nutrients still further. (See Hall, 1980.)

Street drugs

These may bring temporary relief from the symptoms of schizophrenia, but addiction may exacerbate the condition; there is plenty of anecdotal evidence that this is so. H. Ashton (1982) says that 'the effects of cannabis have many similarities with the clinical condition [of schizophrenia]', and quotes the following from a paper by W. D. M. Paton (1979) and other workers:

- Fragmentation of thought, distractibility, inability to select relevant material, preservation
- Impairment of recent memory
- Confusion, disassociation, depersonalization
- Paranoid thought, intense anxiety
- Abrupt mood fluctuation
- Incongruity of affect – laughing or weeping without cause
- Free visual imagery, hallucinations (on high doses)
- Withdrawnness, preoccupation with the internal state

Paton concluded that 'any subject could be made to pass into a schizophrenia-like state with an appropriate dose of cannabis'. Ashton comments that 'many cases have been reported in which the use of cannabis caused a recurrence of acute psychotic symptoms [even] in schizophrenic patients well controlled with neuroleptics, because cannabis, like LSD and amphetamines, seems to constitute a special risk for schizophrenics'. The biochemistry of schizophrenics seems to make them especially susceptible to becoming addicts.

Dietary guidelines

As I said at the beginning of this chapter, scientific knowledge is not yet advanced enough to state categorically that diet has a major effect on schizophrenia. But the suggestions are there, and in the meantime it can do no harm – and may do much good – for patients to follow these basic guidelines for healthy living. Anecdotally a number of our members have benefited from an effort to help themselves by dietary manipulations. It is quite a hard task. A grain-free, milk-free diet might help some patients but I have discussed the difficulties of embarking on such a diet.

- No alcohol
- No smoking if possible
- No street drugs
- Take a general vitamin/mineral supplement
- Eat good food such as plenty of fruit and vegetables, chicken, fish, meat and eggs

● Avoid caffeine-containing drinks like tea, coffee and cola – stick to water and fruit juice
● Low blood sugar may increase symptoms, so always keep a healthy snack with you even when you go to bed
● Take plenty of exercise in the fresh air
● Go to bed very early and never get overtired or hungry.

It is probable that a sub-group of schizophrenics may be sensitive to milk and grains. This group may be the paranoid group and according to Dr Chris Reading, those who are sensitive to wheat may be those families who have a tendency to develop pernicious anaemia. I was most gratified recently when a consultant psychiatrist, of his own volition, prescribed a course of injections of vitamin B12 together with tablets of folic acid, to a stable medicated formerly paranoid patient. Many patients might be helped if their consultants did this.

You may wonder why I have not advocated a particular diet in this section of the book. Why have I not recommended a grain-free, milk-free diet? It is because we have not yet got the proof that would enable me to make firm recommendations however much I would like to be able to do so. I hope that patients and their families will glean what they can from the book and experiment if they feel inclined. There are many books available which give gluten-free (grain-free) recipes, and often milk-free.

If we can have the satisfaction of finding out that even one group of schizophrenics, the paranoid form, has a disease of the gut we can give it another name and make it an infinitely more acceptable disease. Quite possibly all groups of schizophrenia will respond to a dietary approach. I fervently hope so.

Conclusions

What we do know is that untreated schizophrenic patients often look malnourished. We know of the frequent dramatic weight loss at the start of their illness. If they are short of a wide range of nutrients because of a malabsorption syndrome, any deficiencies should be made good.

Pinel, in thinking that the primary seat of insanity generally was in the region of the stomach and intestine, was almost certainly right, but advances in this area have been very slow to develop. The brain is still *all* important to the majority of the researchers. They see hallucinations as being diagnostically important and fail to see that these may be ephemeral symptoms caused possibly by these opioid-like peptides derived from food. In the forefront of my mind are all those many replies to the Schizophrenia Association of Great Britain's questionnaire about the presence of digestive symptoms amongst many schizophrenics, starting so often in babyhood, before schizophrenia was thought to be a remote possibility. To what extent, I wonder, were the constant stuffy noses and the clearing of throats, tonsil troubles and appendicitis and severe viral and bacterial infections relevant to the development of the schizophrenia in those who suffered such symptoms prior to their schizophrenia? Were they related to the ingestion of grains and milk? We cannot forget Buscaino's findings of actual damage to the schizophrenic gut in schizophrenia in the pre-neurological era, similar to that now found in coeliac disease. It is important, too, to consider Baruk's ability to cure a 'schizophrenic illness' of long-standing by curing a bacillus coli infection with an anti-toxin. I wonder frequently if a schizophrenic's often severe susceptibility to viral and bacterial infections could be caused because a damaged gut allowed such micro-organisms to pass into the blood in unacceptably high numbers. Animals fed diets of casein, protein, or gluten proteins from wheat were found to be highly susceptible to infection when inoculated with bacteria. The mortality rate was very high.

I think again of the very unexpected improvement of mental health in paranoid schizophrenics when treated with antibiotics and wonder whether such agents could not be investigated as treatments for schizophrenia. The gut flora may need to be examined in schizophrenia. If there is faulty metabolism of foods, are the wrong bacteria, and fungi perhaps, wreaking further havoc? The non-beneficial organisms, including yeasts, may flourish at the expense of the beneficial organisms.

Again I would like to stress the possibility that there may be a malabsorption syndrome in schizophrenia, particularly perhaps in a sub-group of patients whose illness may be related to coeliac disease. The nutritional state of all patients should be examined and deficiencies made good.

References

ABRAHAMSON and PEZET, *Body, Mind and Sugar*. Pyramid, New York, 1971.

ASHTON, Heather, 'Actions of cannabis: do they shed light on schizophrenia?' in Hemmings, Gwynneth (ed) *Biological Aspects of Schizophrenia and Addiction*, Chichester, John Wiley & Sons, 1982.

BERGLAND, R., *The Fabric of Mind*. Viking-Penguin, New York, 1985.

BUSCAINO, G. A., 'The amino-hepato-entero-toxic theory of schizophrenia: an historical evaluation' in *Biological Basis of Schizophrenia* (ed. Hemmings, W. A. and Hemmings, Gwynneth). MTP Press, Lancaster, 1978.

CARNEY, M. W. P., 'Investigations into serum folate and B12 concentrations in psychiatric in-patients with particular reference to schizophrenia' in *Biological Basis of Schizophrenia* (eds. Hemmings, W. A. and Hemmings, Gwynneth). MTP Press, Lancaster, 1978.

COTT, Alan, (1971) 'Controlled Fasting Treatment of Schizophrenia in the USSR', *Schizophrenia*, vol. 13, no. 1. American Schizophrenia Association.

CRAMMER, J. L., 'Trace metals in mental illness', paper given at Schizophrenia Association of Great Britain Conference, London, 1982.

DOHAN, F. C., 'Cereals and schizophrenia: data and hypothesis' in *Acta. Psychiat. Scand.*, 42, 125 (1966).

DOHAN, F. C., 'Schizophrenia: possible relationship to cereal grains and coeliac disease', in *Schizophrenia: Current Concepts and Research* (ed. Sankar, S. PJD Publications Ltd, Hickville (New York), 1969.

HALL, G. M., 'The pharmacology of tobacco smoking in relation to schizophrenia' in *The Biochemistry of Schizophrenia and Addiction* Hemmings, Gwynneth (ed). MPT Press, Lancaster, 1980.

NIEKOFF, Arthur, *Food, Science and Society*. Nutrition Foundation Inc., New York, c.1970.

PATON, W. D. M., Concluding summary in Nahas, G. G. and Paton, W. D. M. (eds.) Pergamon, Oxford, 1979.

PFEIFFER, Carl C., 'Behavioural toxicology – heavy metals affecting behaviour' in *Psychopharmacology Bulletin*, vol. 14, no. 3 (1978).

PHILPOTT, W., Lecture presented to American, Canadian and British Schizophrenia Associations, London, September 1971.

SOURKES, T. L., *Biochemistry of Mental Disease*. Harper and Row, New York, 1962.

VADDADI, K. S., COURTNEY, P., GILLEARD, C. J., MANKU, M. S. and HORROBIN, D. F., 'A double blind trial of essential fatty acid supplementation on abnormal movements, psychiatric states and memory in patients with tardive dyskinesia', *Psych. Res.*, in press.

Biochemistry of Mental Disorders. World Health Organization, Geneva, 1969.

Biological Research in Schizophrenia. World Health Organization, Geneva, 1970.

8

REHABILITATION

Digging for victory over mental illness

Not so long ago a middle-aged man came to see me at the SAGB's headquarters in Bangor. He was now a successful farmer, but in his youth, before the advent of neuroleptic drugs, he had had to be treated for mental illness in hospital – whether or not it was schizophrenia was unknown. My visitor told me that he and his fellow patients worked hard and long in the farm and garden of the hospital. They returned in the evening to plenty of good wholesome food and went to bed physically tired but very content. Next day, having slept soundly, they awoke refreshed and ready for another day's satisfying toil. Under this regime, the farmer told me, his health improved greatly and he was eventually discharged. I think there are lessons to be learnt here: such a simple, healthy way of life would not on its own effect a cure for most schizophrenics, but it would probably be very beneficial for them.

What is rehabilitation?

One definition of rehabilitation has been provided by W. A. Anthony and R. P. Liberman (1986), who write: 'The overall goal of psychiatric rehabilitation is to assume that a person with a psychiatric disability can perform those physical, emotional, social and intellectual skills needed to live, learn and work in the community with the least amount of support necessary, from agents of the helping professions.' They quoted H. R. Lamb

(1982) as saying that 'work therapy geared to the capability of the individual patient should be the cornerstone of community treatment of the long-term patient'.

I disagree with the idea of 'the *least* support' from medical and social workers; I think discharged patients need readily available, friendly medical supervision such as was made available – despite many logistical shortcomings – in the Israeli hospital mentioned in Chapter 4. Doctors should feel they have a continuing responsibility that does not end when voluntary patients are discharged, or discharge themselves. Additionally, the most important aspect of all has been passed over by these authors: the patient must be in a reasonable state of mental well-being before he can participate in vocational schemes. The hospital regime described by the farmer, in which the patients worked hard at a therapeutic occupation but had medical help quickly available when needed because they were still in hospital, addressed the situation far better – and that was some forty years ago!

Where community care falls down

A recent television documentary about a Scandinavian scheme for looking after the mentally ill impressed me greatly: it seemed much better than anything currently available in Britain. The hospital grounds housed residential and work units offering discharged patients work of different degrees of complexity. They also had the opportunity of going back to the hospital if they wanted to, where they would be given the sick role and cared for completely.

Ideally, Britain's big psychiatric hospitals should not be closed but should be modernized and fitted with first-class pathology laboratories. The grounds and gardens could once again become hives of industry, as patients who would otherwise be discharged into a cold and unfriendly world recovered their health gradually. Well-meaning people argue that the proceeds from the sale of the hospitals can be channelled into community care – but what sort of community care, and how long will the money last?

How will the doctors, nurses and social workers function when their workplaces are shut down? The truth is that 95 per cent of psychiatric hospital in-patients are there of their own volition, and no one has any legal responsibility for them once they leave hospital. Many become lost to the system, migrating to large cities where anonymity and loneliness make their lives utterly desolate. No medical teams will be able to trace them there.

An NIMH leaflet published in 1986 defined rehabilitation as including

> a wide array of non-medical interventions for those with schizo-phrenia. Rehabilitation programmes emhasise social and voca-tional training to help patients and former patients overcome difficulties in these areas. Programmes may include vocational counselling, job training, problem-solving and money man-agement skills, use of public transportation and social skills training. These approaches are important for the success of the community-centred treatment of schizophrenics, because they provide discharged patients with the skills necessary to lead pro-ductive lives outside the sheltered confines of a mental hospital.

This is great news for a few patients – those who can be accom-modated by such well-intentioned schemes. But most of those out in the community are released when still full of symptoms; don't have loving, responsible families; won't have been helped in this way; and have to manage miserably on their own. They are bad with money, and alienate landladies; often dirty and ill-clad, all too quickly some become dependent on alcohol and drugs.

Moves to return to proven old methods

Derek McClure of the Industrial Therapy Organization, a North-ern Ireland company, gave a most encouraging talk at a Mental Health Foundation (MHF) meeting in 1987. The company has set up a number of work schemes and is run on a commercial basis. He described how, with an MHF grant, they were able to start growing plants for the production of dried flowers; the statutory authorities had declined to make any money available because they felt that the task was beyond the capabilities of mentally ill people. The venture had gone from strength to strength and had diversified into Christmas trees, which previously had been imported from the Netherlands. The work was, said Mr McClure, very labour-intensive, and three-quarters of the workforce were schizophrenics.

Similar excellent schemes have been started up elsewhere. The Rudolph Steiner organization uses farming as therapy for young people, who are responsible for the whole process from sowing crops to baking bread; they also learn weaving and other skilled creative activities. Music forms an important part of their curriculum.

An SAGB member in Australia wrote to me about her son, whose psychiatrist had told him he would never work again. But he was responding well to his medication and had been working for some years in a garden centre, where the rhythm of the seasons and the routine of the physical work benefited him greatly. He no longer suffered from paranoia, and had stopped thinking that people were evil. Clearly, healthy physical labour out of doors works wonders for a large number of mentally ill people.

Rehabilitation in other countries

Different countries and different cultures have varying attitudes to the mentally ill members of their society. Some of their approaches to rehabilitation contain lessons for Britain.

In Israel, no person's case is ever dropped. Contact is maintained with most schizophrenics for the rest of their lives, and medical help is always available in times of stress. Sweden has an enlightened policy, but – surprisingly – appears to neglect nutrition. Assistance is given with housing, employment and leisure activities. Patients may visit the hospital ward occasionally, or return there for a new rehabilitation course. The Spanish start work therapy early and treat it seriously: it is not just a time-filler, but must have meaning for the worker – who is always paid for what he does – and result in a marketable product. Patients and staff are organized into 'artisan co-operatives', and work is given to patients on the basis of their interests and skills rather than in relation to their diagnosis or the results of psychological tests.

If adequate therapy is given at the same time, this approach too would seem to be very enlightened.

Employment of schizophrenics in Britain

Poor medication and the side-effects experienced even when medication is well prescribed can make schizophrenics unsuitable employees in many occupations. Some patients say they lack self-esteem and may therefore present themselves badly – they find it hard to look into a potential employer's eyes when being interviewed; others find the interview process difficult when they are depressed. Even if they do get their job, they may feel very restless or very sleepy – neither situation is conducive to concentration. Impaired vision because of anti-parkinsonian drugs may affect the patient's ability to drive or to operate machinery. Negative symptoms, such as lack of motivation and inertia, are often not touched by medication. Schizophrenics may also be suspicious of their colleagues if their paranoia is not adequately controlled. Obviously some occupations are much more suitable than others for people in this situation: work in shops and libraries, house decorating and general repair work, for instance, might be considered suitable for reasonably well patients. Some find part-time work reduces the demands made on them and is therefore better; others avoid night work because it upsets their regular sleep rhythm; and yet others feel that any job that involves deadlines or piecework is inappropriate.

A recent report by David Clutterbuck concerning employment of the mentally ill says that 'rehabilitation workers are now teaching people [with schizophrenia] to look busy – just as "normal" employees do when they stretch their work out.' It seems very bad advice to encourage former patients to give less than their best when they get a job. The report goes on to say that because of employment difficulties 'organisations representing the mentally ill and mentally restored now sometimes advise them to lie about their handicap, or at least to conceal it'. It is widely recognized that if job applicants reveal a history of mental illness they are less likely to get a job; this is probably because of the stigma attached to mental illness and also because employers know, from past experience, that people with a history of psychiatric disorder are often less dependable.

Mr Brian Davy asked if members of the Schizophrenia Association of Great Britain would answer a questionnaire on graduate employment after mental illnes.

They were asked whether they would reveal the fact of their illness on application forms when seeking employment. Of the respondents nine said they did reveal their psychiatric record; thirteen said they did not and twelve did sometimes. The responses were fairly evenly divided. Clearly, if the illness still exists or is thought to be recurrent, the practical problems of concealment are that much greater. 'A further issue,' wrote Mr Davey, 'is an ethical one – *should* one disclose? It is not going to help one's psychological well-being if one acts against one's ethical principles and/or lives under the shadow of being found out.' Ethics apart, one respondent made a very practical point: 'An employer who offers you a job in full knowledge of your medical problems is likely to provide the working environment most suitable for coping with the problem.'

Surely that is the best solution – not for ex-patients to consider deceiving a future employer at interview, but for employers to aim to provide the ex-patient with more suitable conditions. This might mean letting the employee work for just a short period each day, until his concentration fails, and then giving him time to rest and relax before picking up the threads again.

At one SAGB meeting the Danish psychiatrist Dr Axel Randrup made the point that

> the working power of the schizophrenic, even if it is only partial, should be utilised. That would give a chance for some patients to choose if they want to work (and I think many would want to) and it would also be a considerable economic gain . . . I really think there are opportunities, but it requires a different approach from the employer. You should not require the same thing from an ill person. You should think this man or this woman can do this, or you can expect this and then arrange the pay according to a reasonable standard.

Unfortunately, this rarely happens. Brian Davey's questionnaire also asked about employment of graduates after mental illness. Only about a third of those who responded had been able to find graduate-type jobs; some had been sacked, or had resigned, because symptoms or side-effects had reduced their effectiveness. A study by Nancy Wansbrough and Philip Cooper, quoted by Brian Davey, examined the type of complaints made by employers of the mentally ill: 'Most frequently mentioned were complaints of slow work or odd behaviour . . . sickness absence was also a frequent cause of complaint, usually third in the ranking order.' Mr Davey mentioned that in these days of high unemployment many people's recovery from mental illness is hampered by being discharged from hospital on to the dole, rather than back into a job.

Can we change public attitudes?

Unemployment, and the resultant diminished opportunities for discharged patients to find jobs, are the result of government policies. But there is still much that can be done to help the plight of schizophrenics on the part of individual members of society. The US Rehabilitation Act of 1973 uses these words to define the problem: 'The negative attitudes of the public – constructed by superstition and even more seriously hampered by prejudice and misinformation – become a barrier to potential solutions and cloud the realisation of the magnitude of the problems confronting people troubled by mental illness.'

Like all prejudice, that surrounding mental illness is grounded in a little truth, but down the centuries attitudes have become warped. We are frightened of mental illness because it represents the unknown, and we are particularly frightened of schizophrenia because of the violence that so often attends it. Add to that the fact that it is an inherited condition, and the fear becomes deeply entrenched.

Research and education are the only answers. Once research has finally revealed the biochemical cause and treatment of schizophrenia, that element of the unknown will be removed. Educational programmes dealing with the physical nature of mental illness should be carried out in workplaces and particularly in schools. Children start their lives without prejudices; they are receptive to new ideas, and willing to learn if the knowledge is presented in the right way.

Our brave new world has to be based on knowledge of ourselves and our chemical make-up. When we are prepared to accept the hand dealt us in the genetic draw, then, whether it is a hard or an easy one to play, we must do our best with it. Above all, we must learn to be compassionate to others, particularly those with the potential for developing an inherited disease like schizophrenia.

References

ANTHONY, William A. and LIBERMAN, R. P., 'The practice of psychiatric rehabilitation: historical, conceptual and research base', in *Schizophrenia Bulletin*, vol. 12, no. 4 (1986).

LAMB, H. R., *Treating the Long-term Mentally Ill*. Josey-Bass, San Francisco, 1982.

TIMMS, Philip P. W., 'Schizophrenia, homelessness and asylum', talk given to All-Parliamentary Group on Mental Health, 29.11.88.

WARNER, Richard, *Recovery from Schizophrenia*. Routledge and Kegan Paul, London, 1985.

APPENDIX 1

Additional reading on immunology and nutrition:–

BROSTOFF, J. & GAMLIN, L. (1989): *The Complete Guide to Food Allergy and Intolerance*. London, Bloomsbury.
DAVIS, S. & STEWART, ALAN (1987): *Nutritional Medicine*. London, Pan Books.
*GOTTSCHALL, ELAINE (1986): *Food and the Gut Reaction*. Ontario, Canada, Kirkton Press. Order from SAGB.
*WORKMAN, E., HUNTER, J. & JONES, VIRGINIA ALAN (1984): *The Allergy Diet*. London, Dunitz.

*Recipes included.

APPENDIX 2

The Schizophrenia Association of Great Britain (SAGB) has its headquarters at the International Schizophrenia Centre, Bryn Hyfryd, The Crescent, Bangor, Gwynedd LL57 2AG. Telephone (0248) 354048. Anyone interested in becoming a member can write in or telephone and we will send an information pack and attempt to answer specific individual inquiries.

The SAGB has initiated and is funding a major programme of research into the biochemistry of schizophrenia in the department of Biochemistry, University College of North Wales, Bangor, under the directon of Professor J. W. Payne and Dr Islwyn Davies. The first studies encompass an investigation of gut permeability in schizophrenics, in their close family member and in controls, and a study of the effects of neuroleptics on gut permeability. Other work is being pursued using cell culture and other techniques.

From October 1st 1989 the Association is leasing three floors of laboratories from UCNW as an Institute of Biological Psychiatry, certainly unique in this country and possibly in the world. Research here will be patient-oriented. Families who have a schizophrenic member will be able to come to Bangor from anywhere in the world to be assessed biochemically and to take part in the basic research studies, which are expected to encompass genetic studies. Already families come to Bangor to take part in the research, giving blood and urine samples. Part of this blood is sent to the District General Hospital for routine biochemical screening through the kind co-operation of the staff in the chemical pathology department.

For the successful working of the Institute we still need *a very great deal of money* – about £5 million in all – and if any readers organize fund-raising events to that end, we will be very grateful indeed. Please help if you can. The need to solve the problem of schizophrenia is very great. The burden of suffering it brings is intolerable. The researchers at the Institute will be considering schizophrenia as the whole body disease that we in SAGB believe it to be.

APPENDIX 3

The Association has published three books of the Proceedings of Conferences. These are:–

BIOLOGICAL BASIS OF SCHIZOPHRENIA (1978): Hemmings, W. A. & Hemmings, Gwynneth (eds.) Lancaster, MTP Press. £19.50
BIOCHEMISTRY OF SCHIZOPHRENIA & ADDICTION (1980): Hemmings, Gwynneth (ed.) Lancaster, MTP Press.
BIOLOGICAL ASPECTS OF SCHIZOPHRENIA & ADDICTION (1982): Hemmings, Gwynneth (ed.) Chichester. John Wiley & Sons. £19.50

SAGB holds small stocks of *The Biological Basis of Schizophrenia* and of *Biological Aspects of Schizophrenia & Addiction*, and will sell these as long as stocks last.
The Biochemistry of Schizophrenia & Addiction could probably be obtained from the library, as it is now sold out.